ALL ABOUT
SCIENCE FAIRS

by John and Patty Carratello
Illustrated by Anna Chellton

W9-CNB-077

Teacher Created Materials, Inc.
P.O. Box 1040
Huntington Beach, CA 92647
©1989 Teacher Created Materials, Inc.
Made in U.S.A.

ISBN 1-55734-228-8

All About *Science Fairs*

TABLE OF CONTENTS

INTRODUCTION 4

TEACHER'S GUIDE 5

PARENT'S PACKET

A Letter To Parents 17

Do's and Don'ts 18

Science Project Completion Schedule 19

Parent's Evaluation 20

STUDENT HANDBOOK

The Science Fair Comic Book 21

STUDENT WORKSHEETS

QUESTION

Things I Would Like To Know More About! 40

Many Ways To Ask! 41

Can I Do It Myself? 42

I Have Questions (House) 43

I Have Questions (Books) 44

I Have Questions (Television) 45

I Have Questions (Myself) 46

Narrow It Down! 47

My Best Question! 48

Make It Clear! 49

Science Project Ideas — Level 1 50

Science Project Ideas — Level 2 51

Science Project Ideas — Level 3 52

Polishing My Question! 53

My Question! 54

HYPOTHESIS

Dear Diary 55

My Journal (Title Page) 56

My Journal (Research Entry) 57

My Journal (Test Entry) 58

My Journal (General Entry) 59

What Next? 60

What Was The Question? 62

I Predict! 63

I Think 64

Table of Contents (Continued)

PROCEDURE
    Materials List 65
    Control! 66
    Order! 67
    Peanut Butter And Jelly 68
    Testing: 1, 2, 3 69
    Science Safety 70
    Working With Animals 71
    Make A Record 72
    Just Average 73
    I Propose 74
RESULTS
    Put It In Writing! 76
    Read A Line Graph 77
    Make A Line Graph 78
    Read A Bar Graph 79
    Make A Bar Graph 80
CONCLUSION
    In Conclusion 81
REPORT
    Science Project Report 82
ORAL PRESENTATION
    My Oral Presentation 84
DISPLAY BOARD
    Make Them Look! 85
    Show And Tell 86
    Science Project Identification 89
    Science Project Identification Tags 90
    Maintenance Agreement 91
EVALUATION
    My Science Project Evaluation 92
GRIDS
    Half Inch 93
    Quarter Inch 94
    Centimeter 95
    Half Centimeter 96

All About

INTRODUCTION

The world of today and tomorrow has one predominant characteristic — CHANGE! And whenever there is change, one must be able to adapt to the change. One must be able to sense and clarify problems, as well as find solutions to those problems.

This is exactly what science fairs are all about! Participation in a science fair gives children the opportunity to develop the skills, attitudes, and knowledge that will help them be comfortable with — and successful in — their ever changing world.

All About Science Fairs is a very **practical** guide to helping children plan, complete, and present their science fair projects. It provides a sequential program of skill-building activities, designed to give students valuable practice in mastering each step of the **scientific method**. It also provides tips on how to construct an eye-catching display board and how to give an oral presentation. A reproducible comic book-style story — *The Science Fair Comic Book* — introduces children and their parents to the basic elements of a science fair project, and reinforces the concepts being taught in the classroom.

All About Science Fairs is a must for teachers who want their students to get the maximum value out of participating in a science fair.

TEACHER'S GUIDE

Several months before your school's science fair, send home with each student a packet of science fair materials, which should include A LETTER TO PARENTS, DO'S AND DON'TS, SCIENCE PROJECT COMPLETION SCHEDULE (fill in dates), PARENT'S EVALUATION, as well as any other materials you may want parents to have. These materials will help parents understand their role in making their child's science fair experience a rewarding one.

Distribute THE SCIENCE FAIR COMIC BOOK in class. Take a few days to read and discuss it with your students. Then, have them put their names on their books and take them home. If they color their books, remind them not to color over the words!

Note: You may want to hold a comic book coloring contest. This could be a contest for an individual class, a grade level, or an entire school. You may want to announce the winners on the day of the science fair, as an added attraction!

LEARNING OBJECTIVES

The objectives in this guide may be used in any way. They may be divided into smaller objectives, combined, eliminated, or supplemented with other materials.

The activities suggested for the objectives are both **oral and written.** Some activities may be sent home so that parents may work together with their children.

In presenting the learning objectives, **paraphrase the student information** to match the level of your students. The student information is given in *italic* print.

Write down important words on the chalkboard as they are introduced.

OBJECTIVE: PRACTICE ASKING QUESTIONS.

*When we read **THE SCIENCE FAIR COMIC BOOK**, you learned what a **science project** is — an **investigation** you do to find the answer to a question you have!*
*Today we will start at the very beginning of the science project process. Over the next few months you will have a chance to **practice each step** in doing a science project, as you work on your **own** project.*
Can anyone tell me what the first step in doing a science project is? (Ask a question about something you can investigate.)

Place an object where students can see it. Objects used may be common items such as a can of shaving cream, a telephone, a stapler, a musical instrument, or even a pencil.

Let's practice asking questions! Can anyone here ask a question about this? (Refer to the object.)

As students begin to ask questions, encourage them to ask more questions. Questions should lead to even more and more questions.

For Example:

What does it do? How was it made? Why does it grow the way it does? Why is part of it colored one way and another part isn't? How does it work? Why would someone invent it? How long does it last? Is it dangerous? Could it be made another way? Could it be made bigger? Could it be made smaller? Could it be made better? Could it be made with different materials? Could it be made to look like something else? Is it affected by temperature? How many ways

can people use it? Can it be used for something it wasn't designed for?

This activity may be done periodically to get the question "juices" flowing.

Another way to do this activity is to divide the class into teams, giving each team an object. Have one person on the team write down all the questions the team can come up with in five minutes. Then, rotate the objects, so that each team gets a chance with each object. Once a team has questioned every object, read the questions to the class. You may want to have the class vote on the most interesting question. Divergent thinking should be encouraged and praised!

Use THINGS I WOULD LIKE TO KNOW MORE ABOUT! (Page 40) as a follow up.

OBJECTIVE: IDENTIFY DIFFERENT WAYS TO ASK A QUESTION.

When you ask a question, you have to ask it so you can get an answer.
There are several ways to ask a question.

1. *You can ask a question that can be answered "yes" or "no."*

For Example:

Are boys stronger than girls? (There may be a reaction to this example.)
Can a caterpillar travel faster than a mealworm?
Is nighttime colder than daytime?

2. *You can ask a question in which a choice is to be made.*

For Example:

Who are stronger — boys or girls?
Which is faster — a caterpillar or a mealworm?
Which is colder — nighttime or daytime?

3. *Or, you can ask a question in which you don't answer "yes" or "no," or make a choice.*

For Example:

How much stronger are boys than girls?
How much faster is a caterpillar than a mealworm?
What is the difference in temperature between nighttime and daytime?

Give students a chance to come up with other examples for each type of question. Don't be concerned with the quality of the questions at this time. Accept anything that meets the objective.

Use MANY WAYS TO ASK! (Page 41) as a follow up.

OBJECTIVE: DISTINGUISH BETWEEN A QUESTION WHICH CAN BE ANSWERED BY ONE'S SELF AND A QUESTION WHICH CAN'T.

I'm going to read you a list of questions. Raise your hand when you hear a question that you can investigate by yourself, without having to look in a book, or ask someone else for the answer. Be ready to tell us how.

If it becomes clear that it would not be possible for the student to investigate a question with the resources available to him or her, ask the class, *"Would this be a good question for a science fair project?"*

1. *Does the moon orbit the Earth?*

2. *Will goldfish eat cooked egg yolk?*

3. *What is the deepest part of the Pacific Ocean?*

4. *How do plants use chlorophyll to make food?*

5. *Does the human tongue have different areas of taste?*

6. *Can loud music affect your heart rate more than soft music?*

7. *Which color gets warmest in sunlight — black, red, or white?*

8. *What is the center of the Earth made of?*

9. *How many people are there in the world?*

10. *What is the shape of the Earth?*

Your question for your science fair project should be one that you can answer by **yourself.** *You want to ask a question for which you don't have to look in a book for the answer — or have to ask someone else for the answer.*

Use CAN I DO IT MYSELF? (Page 42) as a follow up.

Note: Students may disagree on which questions they can answer by themselves. When they have completed the worksheet, find out their reasons. Some students, for example, may actually be able to "discover" the basic principles of aerodynamics, in answer to the question, "How do airplanes fly?" For others, discovering the basic principles of aerodynamics would be as likely as them discovering, "What is the temperature on Venus?"

OBJECTIVE: FIND QUESTIONS TO ASK ABOUT THINGS ONE SEES, DOES, AND THINKS.

I am going to give you a worksheet to take home today.

Use the following worksheets (Pages 43-46) as a series of activities that students can do at home with their parents. Send them home one at a time, after you have explained to the child what it is he or she must do.

I HAVE QUESTIONS ABOUT THINGS I'VE SEEN PEOPLE DO AROUND MY HOUSE

I HAVE QUESTIONS ABOUT THINGS I'VE READ

I HAVE QUESTIONS ABOUT THINGS I'VE SEEN AND HEARD ON TELEVISION

I HAVE QUESTIONS ABOUT THINGS I'VE THOUGHT ABOUT ALL BY MYSELF

OBJECTIVE: NARROW DOWN CHOICES FOR A QUESTION.

By this time, students should have had a good deal of opportunity to think about questions for their projects. You can now help them narrow down their questions to their two favorite ones. Talk over their questions with them individually, or as a group.

Use NARROW IT DOWN! (Page 47) as a follow up.

OBJECTIVE: SELECT A SINGLE QUESTION.

In order for students to select the best question for a science project, they will have to consider the materials they have or can get, as well as the resources (books, magazines, people, etc.) they actually have available to them. You can help them take inventory of their materials and resources, either individually, or as a group.

Use MY BEST QUESTION! (Page 48) as a follow up.

OBJECTIVE: RECOGNIZE A CLEAR QUESTION.

1. Send about 5 to 8 students out of the room, with an assistant who will make sure that they cannot hear what is going on inside. The assistant will stand near the door and will send in one student at a time, as you call for him or her.

2. Make up a set of directions for the student to follow. Remind the rest of the class not to give the student any help.

   For Example:

   Will you please bring me a book and put it on the desk? Thank you.
   Will you please bring me a crayon and put it in my hand? Thank you.
   Will you get a piece of paper and write your name on it? Thank you.
   Will you now fold it? Thank you.
   Will you please put it against the wall and sit down? Thank you.

3. And so on. You may want to add a few things of your own. Just make sure that the directions and the sequence of the directions remain the same for each child.

4. Elicit from the class that each person interpreted the directions a little differently. And, that that is why a person must be clear when he or she wants to say or ask something in a scientific investigation.

Students may, after this exercise, begin to hold you to your exact word when giving them instructions. Make sure that you tell them that when people know each other well, much of what they say is already understood. So when, for example, you ask children to sit down, they know that that means in **their** chairs — not on their desks or on the floor.

Use MAKE IT CLEAR! (Page 49) as a follow up.

OBJECTIVE: WRITE A CLEAR QUESTION.

Discuss students' answers for MAKE IT CLEAR! Tell students that in order to successfully investigate the questions they have selected for their projects, they must be very clear about what they are asking.

Use POLISHING MY QUESTION! (Page 53) as a follow up.

Note: As students complete their questions, have them copy their questions onto MY QUESTION! (Page 54). Cut them out and display them on a bulletin board entitled: WE HAVE A LOT OF QUESTIONS!

The questions first displayed may inspire and/or motivate other students, who have not yet done so, to devise or finalize their own questions. If it doesn't appear that a student will be able to create his or her own question, you may want to either suggest a question, or use the SCIENCE PROJECT IDEAS (Pages 50-52) in this book, matching the question level with the level of the student.

Option 1: You may run off, cut, and put the idea strips in a bowl or a bag. Have the student select one.

Option 2: Run off, cut, and insert the idea strips into fortune cookies. Have the student select a "science fortune cookie."

OBJECTIVE: IDENTIFY WAYS TO RESEARCH A QUESTION BEFORE FORMING A HYPOTHESIS.

So far you have completed the first step in doing a science fair project:

1. Ask a question.

Now, you are ready for the next step — to form a hypothesis. A hypothesis is a good guess about what the answer to your question will probably be. But you don't want to make just any old guess. You want to learn as much about the topic of your question as you possibly can. Then when you make a guess, it will be a good guess, because it will be a smart guess.

Some students won't really have to do any research in order to form a hypothesis for their question. However, they can still benefit from finding out as much as they can about their question's topic.

Finding information about something is called research, because you search for information.

If I wanted to make a carrot cake, and I didn't know how, I could just guess how I might make one — OR I could do research to find out what other people who have already made a lot of carrot cakes have to say. Then I know there would be a good chance that I would make a good carrot cake.

But, how could I find out about making carrot cakes? That is, what could I do to research my question — "How do I make a carrot cake?" (Ask someone, or get the recipe from a book or a magazine.)

If the drain in my sink was clogged, and I wanted to fix it myself, I could just get out my wrenches and guess which pipes to start taking apart — OR I could do research to find out what other people who have already fixed a lot of clogged sinks have to say. Then I know there would be a good chance of my finding and removing the clog from my drain, without having to tear apart the plumbing of my entire house.

But, how could I find out about fixing a clogged drain? That is, what could I do to research my question — "How do I fix a clogged drain?" (Ask someone, call a plumber, or read a book.)

Once you have a clearly-stated question, you should begin to research — find out as much as you can about — the topic of your question. You can read books, magazines, and newspapers. You can talk with your parents, your teacher, or someone else who might know something about your topic. Sometimes computers can also help you get information. Sometimes you can get information from radio, records, cassettes, television, films, or videos. Your own past experience is also very valuable. There are many ways to research the topic of your question.

Give your students sample project questions (see SCIENCE PROJECT IDEAS). Discuss ways they could research the topic area of each question – which resources to explore.

If I wanted to know _____ (insert question), how could I find the information I would need to make a good guess about what the answer will be? That is, what could I do to research my question?

Note: Spend as much time with this objective as you would like. You will, of course, have to adjust what is to be expected of your students, depending upon their level.

If students still need more help in understanding what research is, use **WHAT NEXT?** (Page 60).

1. Go over the directions with them, reminding them that all a hypothesis is is a good guess, and that all research is is a way to learn all that you can before making a guess.

2. Do the worksheet activity.

3. Explain to them the following:

Do you know that you just used research to answer the questions in WHAT NEXT?

What questions, you might ask? These questions (refer to the worksheet): "What will happen when the girl hits the ball with the bat?" "What will happen when the dog sees the cat?" "What will happen when the girl kisses the boy?"

The guesses you made in WHAT NEXT? were based on what you have found out from your own life learning, or life "research." You know that no one is going to hit a baseball into outer space with a bat. You know that a dog and cat aren't going to sit down and read a book together — with glasses on yet! And, you know that a boy won't turn into a frog because he gets kissed by a girl.

But, because there is so much to learn about the world, we can't always depend on our own life learning to know what the answer to a question will be. We have to use the life learning of other people to help us answer our questions. We can find out about what other people have learned by either reading about what they have to say, or by talking or listening to them. And we call that research.

OBJECTIVE: KEEP A WRITTEN RECORD.

Ask individual students what they did two weeks ago on Wednesday afternoon, at exactly 1:30 p.m. The students will most likely not remember.

How could you remember — if you knew someone was going to ask you two weeks from now — what you did today? (Answers will vary.)

You write down what you did!

In a scientific investigation you must write down everything you do and think about every time you work on your investigation. This way others can know how you got the answer to your question. You keep everything you write down in a written record called a journal.

A journal is a lot like a diary. Who knows what a diary is? (Students may or may not know.)

A diary is a personal journal — a written record — of what you do and think about every day.

Draw a diary page on the chalkboard (see DEAR DIARY . . ., Page 55) and model (select an example) what a person (the age of your students) might write in a diary.

Use DEAR DIARY . . . as a follow up.

OBJECTIVE: SELECT THE APPROPRIATE TYPE OF JOURNAL ENTRY.

Writing in your journal is like writing in a diary. But, instead of keeping a record about everything you do and think, you only keep a record of those things that have to do with your investigation.

Both a diary and journal tell a story. And, the story your journal tells begins with your question, and the research you do to find out as much as you can about the topic of your question.

The journal ends when the student has found an answer to his or her question, and writes a conclusion to the investigation.

The first page of your journal is your title page.

Distribute MY JOURNAL (TITLE PAGE) (Page 56) and have your students color the letters. Students may also write the question being investigated on the title page, and draw a picture. The starting date of the journal will be the date of the first entry, and the ending date will be the date of the last entry.

DO NOT HAVE CHILDREN WRITE THEIR NAMES ON THE TITLE PAGE! Since the author of the journal must be anonymous at the time of the fair, put a temporary page for the child's name in front of the title page until it is time for the fair. When the journal is left with the display, the temporary page should be removed and discarded. Once the journal is returned to the child after the fair, the child may write his or her name on the title page.

The other pages you put in your journal will depend on the nature of your **entry.** *An entry is another name for when you go into — or "enter" — your journal to write something down. You enter into your journal like you enter into a room. There are three basic types of entries — research, test, and general.*

These are not standard designations for journal entries. However, distinguishing the types of entries they must make will help students organize their writing. You may not want to use the pages designed to accomodate these entry designations, opting instead to have your students use a regular notebook.

At the beginning of your investigation, when you enter into your journal, it will be to write down the names of the books, magazines, and other things you've read (as well as the names of the people you talked with), and the information you got from them. This is a **research entry.**

Model a few sample entries for your students, using a MY JOURNAL (RESEARCH ENTRY) page (page 57).

You may, depending on the level of your students, want to give students more specific guidelines as to what information to include for "source of information." Also, depending on the level of your students, you may want to discuss the importance of paraphrasing the information from one's source, and putting what isn't paraphrased in quotation marks.

Later, as you get into the testing part of your investigation, you will want to make another kind of entry that includes:

1. *What you* **did** *to test your hypothesis. This might be a restatement of one or more steps in the procedure. Here you may want to indicate what materials were used, as well as the means of observation, such as a clock, scale, ruler, or thermometer.*

2. *What you* **observed** *(changes in time, weight, size, temperature, etc.), as well as the time and/or length of the observation, if that is important. (This is the data that is entered onto the chart the student will make.) Here you may also want to describe the environment in which the observation took place, list which senses were used to make the observation, as well as mention any new discoveries.*

3. *What you* **thought** *about during the test, or after the test. These may be personal thoughts as well, if they are related to the investigation. Here you may want to write down anything that entered your mind as you were working, such as whether or not the pot the water was boiled in was clean before you did your test, or whether or not you had needed more potting soil than you had anticipated.*

This is a **test entry.**

Model a few sample entries for your students, using a MY JOURNAL (TEST ENTRY) page (Page 58).

EXAMPLE 1

What I did:

I counted the number of people in my class with brown hair. Then I counted the number of people in my class with black hair and blonde hair.

What I observed:

Fourteen people have brown hair. Six people have black hair. And, seven people have blonde hair. (There is no need to write in a time for this kind of test.)

What I thought:

It was hard to decide what color certain types of hair really were. Some brown hair was dark enough to look black, and some blonde hair was dark enough to look brown. It's really silly how some people don't like others because of their color.

EXAMPLE 2

What I did:

I poured a tablesoon (15 milliliters) of salt into the pan with water, and stirred the water for 15 seconds with the spoon. I then had my mom put the pan on the stove. I had her turn the heat on high as soon as I started the stopwatch.

What I observed:

The water bubbles began to come to the surface of the water in about 40 seconds. (In this particular test, the student should write down the starting time and the ending time of the test.)

What I thought:

The way the pot was resting on the stove may have changed the time in which it took the water to boil. Is another source of heat better for boiling water?

EXAMPLE 3

What I did:

I put wax on String B and repeated the same message I had transmitted to Jimmy on String A, which didn't have any wax.

What I observed:

Jimmy heard more words in the message correctly than he did when I hadn't waxed the string. (In this test, the student should write down the time the test began and ended. He or she may decide later that the time of day, because of its likely correlation with the temperature outside, may be a variable that needs to be controlled.)

What I thought:

I may have been speaking more clearly when we used the waxed string. If I used a tape recording of my voice instead, I would be sure the sound source was the same each time.

Sometimes you may want to write down other thoughts or ideas you have had about your investigation. You may also want to make a chart, draw a picture, design a new invention, have a place to put photographs, or just doodle. This is a **general entry.**

Model a few sample entries for your students, using a MY JOURNAL (GENERAL ENTRY) page (Page 59).

8

Note: A journal is like a log, but it contains more than just the bare-bones facts that a log contains — reconstructing only the physical aspects of the investigation. A journal is much more interactive, with the scientist telling about his or her biases, value judgements, etc. It is a rambling internal dialogue at times. It includes how the scientist feels about what he or she is doing.

Having students keep a journal is an excellent opportunity for teaching language skills, as well as math and art skills.

Provide students with a "starter" journal — a packet containing copies of each of the three types of the MY JOURNAL entry pages.

Note: When a test takes longer than a day, have the student date each time entry (above or below the clock), as well as circle whether the time entered was in the a.m. or p.m.

See MY JOURNAL (TEST ENTRY).

OBJECTIVE: MATCH A HYPOTHESIS WITH ITS QUESTION.

You should be able to tell what a question was from the way a hypothesis is stated.

Tell me what the question was for the following hypotheses:

1. *Girls can run faster than boys.* (Who can run faster — boys or girls? Or can girls run faster than boys?)

2. *Ants like sweet food better than sour food.* (What kind of food do ants like better — sweet or sour? Or do ants like sweet food better than sour food?)

3. *A bicycle with bigger wheels can go faster than a bicycle with smaller wheels.* (What can go faster — a bicycle with bigger wheels or a bicycle with smaller wheels? Or can a bicycle with bigger wheels go faster than a bicycle with smaller wheels?)

4. *A mealworm can travel 3 inches (about 8 centimeters) in 11 seconds.* (How long does it take for a mealworm to travel 3 inches or about 8 centimeters?)

Use WHAT WAS THE QUESTION? (Page 62) as a follow up.

OBJECTIVE: WRITE A CLEAR HYPOTHESIS.

A clear hypothesis is:

1. *To the point*

2. *Tells what will happen, based on what the question asks*

3. *Follows the noun/verb relationship of the question*

Write the following questions on the board, and have students write a clear hypothesis. Tell them to make believe they have already done their research. What they want to do is write the hypothesis so it follows the criteria above.

Do our bodies give off heat? (Hypothesis: Our bodies give off heat.)
Which apple slice will go the longest time without browning — one that has been dipped in lemon juice, or one that hasn't. (Hypothesis: The apple slice that has been dipped in lemon juice will go the longest time without browning.)

Do other examples as well.

Use I PREDICT! (Page 63) as a follow up.

When I PREDICT! has been collected and discussed, distribute I THINK . . . (Page 64) to your students, in order that each may write a hypothesis for his or her own question.

Tell students that they do not need to begin with the words "I think" — we already know what they think by what they write!

OBJECTIVE: DETERMINE MATERIALS NEEDED IN PLANNING A PROCEDURE.

So far you have completed the following steps in doing a science fair project:

1. *Ask a question.*

2. *Form a hypothesis.*

Now, you are ready for the next step — to plan your procedure.

The first thing you must do in planning your procedure is to determine the materials you will need to carry out your investigation.

If you were going to bake a cake, you would need to make a list of the ingredients you would need, to make sure you had them or to get them if you didn't. You wouldn't want to get into the middle of preparing everything and then discover that you needed something else to complete the job!

But, you can't just buy any old ingredients. You need to know the kind and how much you will need. Sometimes a recipe calls for whole milk, so you can't use powdered milk or non-fat milk.

It's the same thing with a scientific investigation. If you need a certain size jar to carry out your investigation, you don't want to just write down jar. If your investigation requires a certain size jar, then you should write down the exact size of the jar needed on your materials list.

Draw the following list on the chalkboard. Add items if you wish.

SHOPPING LIST

General	Specific
Cereal	_____
Carton of milk	_____
Sandwich	_____
Soup	_____
Juice	_____
Meat	_____

On the board you see a general shopping list. However, if someone were to give me this list, I wouldn't know what to buy. The person who made the list wasn't specific enough about what he or she wanted.

Can anyone tell me how we can be more specific about the items on the list? Let's start with the cereal.

Continue in the same way with the rest of the items on the shopping list.

You need to be just as specific as we have been here with your science project materials list.

Use MATERIALS LIST (Page 65) as a follow up.

OBJECTIVE: IDENTIFY VARIABLES.

Anything that can change or be changed (You may want to use the words "be different or be made different.") *as you test your hypothesis is called a* **variable***. It is called a variable because it can* **vary** *in quality or quantity from one test to the next. When you do your testing, you want to make sure* **everything is the same** *for each test. This is the only way you can be sure that the test will be* **fair***.*

All the things or variables that you **don't** *want to have change (be different) or vary from one test to the next — and which must be* **controlled** *so they don't — are called the* **controlled variables***.*

The **one** *thing or variable you do want to vary or allow to vary - so you can test it — is called the* **manipulated variable***, because you are changing (making different) or* **manipulating** *something in your test.*

The thing that happens or **results** *when you test the manipulated variable is what you* **measure***, so it is called the* **measured variable***.*

EXAMPLE 1

What boils faster — plain tap water or tap water with salt?

In investigating the answer to this question, it wouldn't be fair to boil the plain water in a big pot with the burner on low, and the water with the salt in a small pan with the burner on high. THAT WOULDN'T BE FAIR! Everything, except for what is to be tested, must be controlled. The container should be the same for both tests, as well as the source of heat, the amount of water, and the procedure for doing the test (i.e., the burner must be turned on at the exact same time for both).

Have your students think of more variables that need to be controlled.

The manipulated variable in this instance is the type of water being tested — you want to know which type boils **faster***. So you need to make certain that everything is the same for boiling the plain water as it is for boiling the water with the salt. If it isn't, it's not a fair test.*

EXAMPLE 2

Who can run faster — Jamie or Jean?

In investigating the answer to this question, it wouldn't be fair to have Jamie run in tennis shoes and wear shorts, and have Jean run in boots and wear long pants. THAT WOULDN'T BE FAIR! Everything, except for what is to be tested, must be controlled. The kind of clothes they wear must be the same for both tests, as well as the surface they run on, and the time that they do their running.

Have your students think of more variables that need to be controlled.

The manipulated variable in this instance is the difference between Jamie's physical ability to run and Jean's physical ability to run — you want to see which one has the physical ability to run **faster***. So you need to make certain that everything is the same in testing Jamie's ability and Jean's ability. If it isn't, it's not a fair test.*

Use CONTROL! (Page 66) as a follow up.

Note: Do not confuse the use of the term controlled variable with the term control — a standard of comparison for verifying the findings of an experiment. The authors feel that the approach used in this book, especially for young scientists, is easier to understand and has more general application to the types of investigations children of this age level will be conducting.

OBJECTIVE: DETERMINE LOGICAL SEQUENCE IN GIVING DIRECTIONS.

Ask students to give you directions for how to tie your shoelace, or another simple task.

Every student should get at least one turn.

The point is to do exactly what you are told to do. If a student doesn't give you a clear direction, he or she will know, because you will take every opportunity to do the wrong thing. The next student has an opportunity to clarify the direction.

For Example:

If student says: *"Hold the laces in your hands."*

You can:

1. Hold the laces close to the shoe.

2. Hold the laces with both hands wrapped around them.

3. Hold the left lace with your right hand and right lace with your left hand.

   The next thing you must do in planning your procedure is to give **step-by-step directions** *for how to carry out the testing of your hypothesis.*

   As you have seen, if you don't put your directions in the right order, or if you leave out a step, it becomes difficult for someone to follow your directions.

Use ORDER! (Page 67) as a follow up.

OBJECTIVE: GIVE CLEAR DIRECTIONS FOR CARRYING OUT A PROCEDURE.

When you give (write) step-by-step directions for the procedure of your science investigation, you must be very clear about what you want to say, just as you were in stating both your question and hypothesis.

You need to give clear descriptions of what you have in mind for your procedure, to make sure others "see" the same thing you do.

Put students in small groups. Have them take turns (after you model several times) describing things in the room, without using the actual name of the thing being described. They can use all the senses — sight, smell, touch, sound, and taste —whenever appropriate.

A student has to introduce the selected object (which shouldn't be stared at) by saying, for example, *"I see something, and it is red."* If that isn't enough, the next time (after a guess has been made) the student says, *"I see something, and it is red and round."* Each time, something else is added to clarify the description.

Also, tell students that they need to communicate in the fewest words possible. Show them that the best way to do that is to give the most distinguishing characteristics first.

Tell them that if they give clear directions, in addition to putting the directions in the right order (with all the steps included), that almost anyone should be able to follow their directions.

Use PEANUT BUTTER AND JELLY (Page 68), and TESTING: 1, 2, 3 . . . (Page 69) as a follow up.

Note: When students are about to do TESTING: 1, 2, 3 . . ., tell them to indicate how many times the investigation is to be repeated to make sure that the data they collect is reliable.

Also, this is a good time to go over safety rules, as well as rules for working with animals. See SCIENCE SAFETY (Page 70), and WORKING WITH ANIMALS (Page 71).

OBJECTIVE: MAKE A CHART TO RECORD DATA.

As you carry out the procedure of your investigation you will need to have a way of collecting and organizing the results (data) you get — a way to write them down, or record them. A good way is to make a chart.

Suppose I wanted to know, "Which brand of paper towel absorbs the most water?" I could make a chart like this to record my data:

Copy the following example onto the chalkboard. You may substitute actual brand names if you'd like.

	Test 1	Test 2	Test 3
Brand A			
Brand B			
Brand C			

Does anyone know why I wrote down Test 1, Test 2, and Test 3? (You want to be sure that you get the most accurate measurements possible in your investigation. Doing more than one test provides measurements you can depend on.)

Is there any reason why I chose to only do three tests? (No. But, three times is probably enough for this investigation. You may need to repeat the procedure for some investigations ten times or more before you are satisfied that the results are accurate - so you can depend on them.)

If I did want to repeat the procedure of my investigation ten times, how would I change the chart I am using to collect and organize my data? (Add seven more test columns.)

You may select a student volunteer to make adjustments to the chart on the board.

Now suppose my question is, "Which takes more water — a bath or a shower?" How could I make a chart to help me collect and organize my data?

Allow students to come to the board to draw an appropriate chart. Ask them how many times they would want to repeat the procedure before they were sure the results were dependable. Also ask them how many people they think should be in the test, and draw the chart accordingly.

This would be a good time to review the idea of controlled variables in an investigation. Ask them what has to stay the same in the investigation (the tub, the unit of measurement, where and when they take the measurement, etc.), in order for the test to be fair.

Here is one way the chart could be made:

	Test 1		Test 2		Test 3	
	Bath	Shower	Bath	Shower	Bath	Shower
Person 1						
Person 2						
Person 3						
Person 4						
Person 5						

Use MAKE A RECORD (Page 72) as a follow up.

NOTE: In doing MAKE A RECORD, two or three students may be assigned to one worksheet.

When they do the actual investigation, one student can record while the other two do the tossing.

CAUTION: Be sure that your students understand that the balloons must be tossed gently - NOT THROWN - to prevent possible injury.

Things you may want to discuss are:

1. The variables to be controlled: the size and shape of the balloon, the amount of water in each balloon, the method of throwing and catching the balloon, as well as the person doing the tossing, and the person doing the catching, etc.

2. What is being measured? Where does the measurement start and where does it end?

OBJECTIVE: AVERAGE DATA.

In MAKE A RECORD your students recorded the data they collected in the balloon toss. In doing so, they found out that for each test they did they got a different measurement. It's time, then, to talk about **averaging**.

Averaging reduces the differences between the many measurements taken in a scientific investigation. It summarizes the many measurements into **a single measurement**, which can be considered an accurate respresentation of the results.

Many graphs represent the average measurement instead of the more numerous actual measurements taken. Averaging is a very important concept in carrying out meaningful investigations – investigations in which a procedure is repeated many times in order to establish consistency in the results. **Averaging is a method of control** – it controls for error.

If your students do not yet have the math skills to do their own averaging, you may help them. They can, however – especially with the help of manipulatives – understand the concept.

Prior to the discussion of averaging, write down the following chart, which could have been used for collecting and organizing the data (measurements taken) in the MAKE A RECORD activity.

BALLOON TOSS

Test 1	Test 2	Test 3	Test 4

When you did the balloon toss, you recorded the results of each test. But, each balloon you tossed probably broke at a slightly different distance for each test. Raise your hand if that happened to you. (You will get a lot of affirmative replies.)

How then do you think you can tell whether or not your hypothesis is supported — if you got so many different measurements from the tests you did? (Answers will vary.)

Wouldn't it be nice if all the measurements could take a vote and give you **one** *single measurement? Well, in a way they can!*

If you add all the measurements you got together, then **divide** *the total by the number of times you did the test, you will get an* **average** *measurement — one that represents all the measurements.*

Fill in the following data on the chart you drew. The measurements in this example are in feet. You may convert that to metric measure if you'd like.

BALLOON TOSS

Test 1	Test 2	Test 3	Test 4
12	15	17	16

Proceed to show the students how to add the measurements, and divide the total to get the average measurement. Then, add a section on the chart to write it in.

BALLOON TOSS

Test 1	Test 2	Test 3	Test 4	AVERAGE
12	15	17	16	15

It's a good idea when you make a chart to have a place ready to write in the average of your tests when your testing is over.

Pause before proceeding.

When you ask "How many raisins are there in a box of cereal?", what you are really asking is "What is the average number of raisins between many boxes of the same cereal." Likewise, when you ask "Which brand of cereal has more raisins?", what you are really asking is "What is the average number of raisins in one brand of cereal versus the average number of raisins in each other brand of cereal being compared."

You can't just count the raisins in a single box. That wouldn't be fair, because different individual boxes of cereal of even the same brand will have slightly different numbers of raisins.

Whether or not you want to find out how many raisins are in one brand, or whether you want to compare brands, you have to count the raisins in several boxes for each brand being tested, and average the results. Then, you will have a single measurement you can work with.

Use JUST AVERAGE (Page 73) as a follow up.

OBJECTIVE: PREPARE A SCIENCE PROJECT PROPOSAL.

Before a student actually carries out the steps to his or her procedure, the student should get the project approved by the teacher, as well as by his or her parents, who will "support" the student's efforts in carrying out the investigation. This is a good time to double-check whether or not the steps completed thus far in the investigation are clearly stated, and whether or not the acquisition of materials, or anything else about the investigation are within the capabilities of the student.

Use I PROPOSE (Page 74) as the form for the project proposal.

OBJECTIVE: EXPRESS RESULTS IN WRITTEN FORM.

So far you have completed the following steps in doing a science fair project:

1. Ask a question.

2. Form a hypothesis.

3. Plan a procedure.

Now, you are ready for the next step — express the results.

The results (data collected) of a scientific investigation are usually expressed two ways — in written form and in picture form. Both are summary statements. The written form reports the results with words. The picture form (often a graph) reports the results so the information can be understood at a glance.

Copy the following chart onto the chalkboard. The chart contains the data collected in the balloon toss investigation. Have students express the results in written form.

BALLOON TOSS

Test 1	Test 2	Test 3	Test 4	AVERAGE
12	15	17	16	15

This is what they should come up with:

RESULTS

In Test 1, the balloon was tossed 12 feet before breaking.

In Test 2, the balloon was tossed 15 feet before breaking.

In Test 3, the balloon was tossed 17 feet before breaking.

In Test 4, the balloon was tossed 16 feet before breaking.

The average distance the balloon was tossed before breaking was 15 feet.

If a large number of tests were done, stating the final average alone would be sufficient.

Use PUT IT IN WRITING! (Page 76) as a follow up.

OBJECTIVE: RECOGNIZE A GRAPH.

Bring in different newspapers and magazines enough for the entire class.

Today we will begin to study graphs. Graphs will be an important part of your science fair project. Who can find a graph in one of these newspapers or magazines to show the class what a graph looks like?

Have the volunteer find one and hold it up for others to see.

Who else can find one?

Repeat this until you know that everyone in class can recognize a graph.

When you think everyone in the class knows what a graph is, have them find and cut out as many as they can in a given amount of time. As they bring the graphs to you, display them randomly on a bulletin board called GRAPH IT! The students will then have many ideas to choose from when making their own graphs for their project display boards.

OBJECTIVE: READ A LINE GRAPH.

A graph makes it easy to see the results of your investigation. Because it is a picture, it can show people what you learned at a glance! People are able to find facts quickly and make comparisons.

As you can see by having looked for graphs in the newspapers and magazines, there are different kinds of graphs. Certain kinds of graphs are better at displaying certain kinds of information than others.

The first kind of graph we will study is a line graph.

When To Use

When you want to show how one or more things changed over a period of time, use a line graph.

How It Works

The line graph is a grid made up of two sets of intersecting lines. The lines that go up and down are called the vertical lines. The lines that go across are called the horizontal lines. Both sets of lines have a label to identify what it is they represent. The vertical label normally tells what is being measured (height, weight, color, temperature, number of people, etc.) The horizontal label normally tells when the measurements are taken (most typically in intervals of minutes, hours, days, weeks, months, and years).

*The **data points** (dots) on the grid represent the facts of the data collected. The **lines** connecting the points give the reader an estimate of the measurements between the points.*

*If you have more than one line to display data, each line can be a different color, or a different design (solid single line, dots, broken line, stars, etc.) to make comparisons easier. A **key** at the bottom of the graph tells the reader what each line stands for.*

Draw the following graph on the chalkboard. Give the background information. Then have students use the graph to answer the questions. You may wish to convert inches to centimeters.

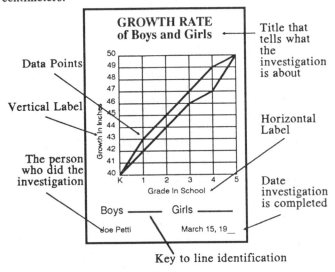

Background Information:

Joe's science project question is, "Do boys grow at the same rate as girls between kindergarten and fifth grade?" He measured 30 boys from each grade and 30 girls. Then he averaged the heights of the boys and the heights of the girls to come up with two representative measurements for each grade. Finally, to more easily see the results of his investigation, he made a line graph.

Questions:

1. *What is the graph about?*

2. *What was measured?*

3. *When were the measurements taken? (In this case, Joe didn't conduct a 5-year study of the same students. He did, however, take a representative sampling from each grade. Therefore, since the measurements **do** represent the growth pattern for children at each grade level, your students may answer that the measurements were "taken" every year.)*

4. *How many inches (centimeters) did the boys grow between the fourth grade and the fifth grade? How many inches (centimeters) did the girls grow in the same time?*

5. *Does Joe's graph provide the information he needs to answer his question?*

Use READ A LINE GRAPH (Page 77) as a follow up.

OBJECTIVE: MAKE A LINE GRAPH.

Draw the following chart and "blank" graph on the chalkboard. Give the background information. Then have students use the data on the chart to complete the graph. Be sure to have them

label both the vertical and horizontal sides of the graph, plot the data points, then connect them.

GIRLS' GROWTH

Grade	Height in Inches
5	50 inches
4	47 inches
3	46 inches
2	44 inches
1	42 inches
K	40 inches

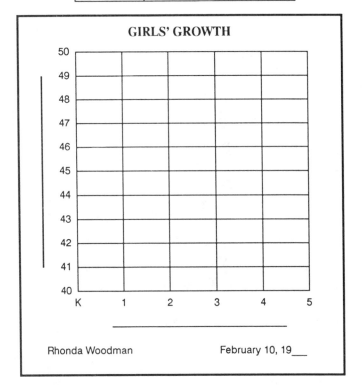

Background Information:

Rhonda's science project question is, "Between which two grades do girls grow the most in height?" She collected her data, then made a chart to show the average growth for each grade. However, she also wants to show the results of her investigation on a line graph.

Use MAKE A LINE GRAPH (Page 78) as a follow up.

OBJECTIVE: READ A BAR GRAPH.

So far we have learned about line graphs. When you want to show how one or more things changed over a period of time, you use a line graph.

Another type of graph is a bar graph.

When To Use

*When you want to show how **totals** compare in things such as weight, distance, time, temperature, depth, and length, use a **bar graph**.*

How It Works

The bar graph is most easily planned out and drawn on a grid. The bars may go either vertically or horizontally, depending upon what it is you are graphing. If you are comparing running distances, go horizontally. If you are comparing the heights of plants, go vertically. A graph is a picture, and when it can suggest a **visual association** to the subject being graphed, as well as a **representation of the data,** then utilize that association.

The labels on the sides of the graph tell what is being compared and how many (or how much) there are of each.

Sometimes you may want to group bars together. Bars grouped together should be distinguished from one another by a difference in color or design, such as vertical lines, horizontal lines, diagonal lines, or dots within the bars themselves. This makes comparisons easier. A **key** at the bottom or top of the graph tells the reader what each bar stands for.

Draw the following graph on the chalkboard. Give the background information. Then have students use the graph to answer the questions.

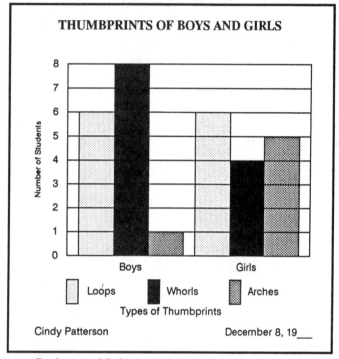

Background Information:

Cindy's science project question is, "What is the distribution of loops, whorls, and arches on thumbprints for the girls and boys in my class?" She took everyone's right thumbprint and made a total of each type for boys and for girls. Then, to more easily see the results, she made a bar graph.

Questions:

1. *What is the graph about?*

2. *What is being compared?*

3. *How many more whorls do the boys have than the girls?*

4. *How many more arches do the girls have than the boys?*

5. *Does Cindy's graph provide the information she needs to answer her question?*

Use READ A BAR GRAPH (Page 79) as a follow up.

OBJECTIVE: MAKE A BAR GRAPH.

Draw the following chart and "blank" graph on the chalkboard. Give the background information. Then have students use the data from the chart to complete the graph. Be sure to have them label both the vertical and horizontal sides of the graph. Then have them plan out the length, width, and spacing of the bars on the grid, before filling them in.

TYPES OF THUMBPRINTS IN THE CLASS

NAME	TYPE	NAME	TYPE
Cindy	Whorl	Jacob	Loop
Marty	Whorl	Nicky	Whorl
John	Arch	Carmen	Loop
Anna	Arch	Misha	Loop
Michael	Loop	Felis	Arch
Jesse	Whorl	Tony	Loop
Paul	Loop	Ylan	Whorl
Hue	Loop	Wendy	Arch
Astrid	Arch	Quinton	Whorl
Marissa	Whorl	Billy	Loop
Darlene	Loop	Christina	Loop
Issac	Whorl	Patty	Whorl
Gail	Arch	Mark	Whorl
Monique	Loop	Bryan	Whorl
Tim	Whorl	Chesica	Loop

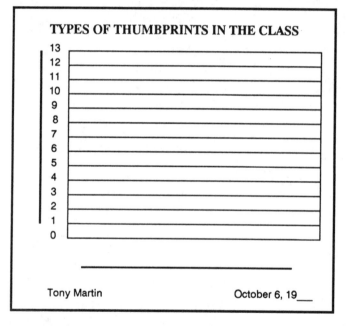

Background Information:

Tony's science project question is, "Do the students in my class have more whorls, loops, or arches on their thumbprints?" He collected his data on a chart. But, now he has decided he also wants to show the information on a bar graph, which would make the information easier to see.

Use MAKE A BAR GRAPH (Page 80) as a follow up.

OBJECTIVE: RECOGNIZE OTHER TYPES OF GRAPHS.

*There are other types of graphs that can be used in addition to line graphs and bar graphs. They are **circle (pie) graphs** and **picture** graphs.*

*A **circle graph** is used to show the parts of a whole. It is sometimes called a **pie graph** because the whole circle, or pie is "cut" into sections.*

Use the following example to discuss the type of science project question that can use a circle graph to illustrate the results of the investigation. Refer to any examples you may also have on your bulletin board.

Question:

What color hair do the students in my class have?

*A **picture graph** uses symbols to represent data.*

Use the following example to discuss the type of science investigation that can use a picture graph to illustrate the results of the investigation. Refer to any examples you may also have on your bulletin board.

Question:

Which brand of paper towel holds the most water?

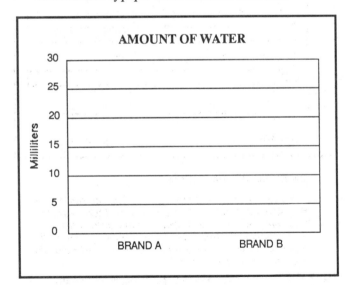

Note: Tell students that photographs, drawings, models, as well as other illustrations can also be used to help people "see" what the student has learned in his or her investigation.

OBJECTIVE: STATE A CONCLUSION BASED ON THE RESULTS OF AN INVESTIGATION.

So far you have completed the following steps in doing a science fair project:

1. *Ask a **question**.*

2. *Form a **hypothesis**.*

3. *Plan a **procedure**.*

4. *Express the **results**.*

*Now, you are ready for the final step (at least in the investigation itself) — state a **conclusion**.*

*The conclusion is a statement which tells the outcome of your project. It tells whether your hypothesis is **supported** or **not supported** by the results of your testing.*

NO INVESTIGATION FAILS if you do everything the way you should.

Remind students that the steps they have been following is called the SCIENTIFIC METHOD of investigation (question, hypothesis, procedure, results, conclusion).

*Even if your hypothesis **isn't** supported, you still learned. And **that** is the purpose of doing a scientific investigation, **or** a science fair project.*

*You will, of course, have to revise your hypothesis in your conclusion statement, if your results didn't support your original hypothesis. In that case just revise your hypothesis to match your results. **Do not change your original hypothesis.***

Students can write their conclusion — whether their hypothesis is supported or not — using the following simple outline.

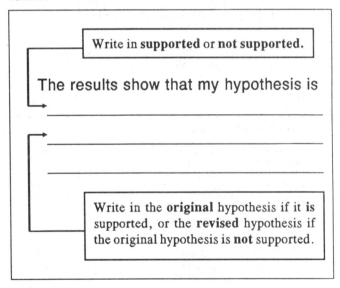

Use IN CONCLUSION . . . (Page 81) as a follow up.

OBJECTIVE: WRITE A SCIENCE PROJECT REPORT.

Now you have completed the following steps in doing a science fair project:

1. *Ask a **question**.*

2. *Form a **hypothesis**.*

3. *Plan a **procedure**.*

4. *Express the* **results.**

5. *State a* **conclusion.**

It is time to make a **report.**

Generally, a scientist's journal is not intended to be public. A report, on the other hand, is a formal paper. It is the written record that is designed to be made public. It is the information that a student puts on his or her science project display board — information about each of the steps followed in the investigation - the **question, hypothesis, procedure, results,** and **conclusion.**

The report should be turned in to the teacher for approval, **prior** to the assignment of a science project display board. This way, all the mechanical "bugs" can be worked out (spelling, grammar, content, and structure) **before** the student transfers the information onto his or her project display board.

Use SCIENCE PROJECT REPORT (Page 82) for the science project report form.

OBJECTIVE: PREPARE TO GIVE AN ORAL PRESENTATION.

Have your students fill out MY ORAL PRESENTATION (Page 84). Tell them to practice it at home. Here are some other suggestions you can give them:

1. **Relax.** *Before you begin, take a deep breath. You will do fine.*

2. **Stand still** *(but not stiff). Don't step from side to side or move around. That distracts from what you are saying.*

3. **Look at your audience** *as you speak.*

4. **Speak loudly enough** *for everyone to hear you, but don't shout.*

5. **Tell what you did.** *Stand to the side of your display and use your hand closest to the display to refer to any part of it that illustrates what you are saying. Point out any interesting features of your project that you want people to especially notice.*

6. **Show your enthusiasm for your project.**

OBJECTIVE: CONSTRUCT A SCIENCE PROJECT DISPLAY.

Doing a science project display helps the student develop communication skills. Constructing a science project display models what a scientist has to do to "market" his or her ideas to get funding for research – to sell the value of the work to others who could benefit from it.

Your science project display should do two things — **show** *and* **tell.**

1. **SHOW —** *The display should catch the viewer's attention so he or she will want to look more closely at your display.*

2. **TELL —** *The display should explain to the viewer what you did and what you learned in your investigation.*

Your **project display board** *is the main part of your display.*

The information that goes on the board is the exact same information that you already put in your science project report, with the addition of any charts, graphs, photographs, or other illustrations that you want to include.

Although your project display board itself is actually sufficient as a self-contained science project display, extra things may be added to make the board even

more interesting to look at, or to further explain what was done in your investigation. Materials, equipment, measuring devices, and demonstrations or explanations of basic principles may be placed in front of the display board. The physical results of the investigation may also be included, if it is both practical and appropriate to do so (sometimes photographs of the results would be better).

Distribute MAKE THEM LOOK! (Page 85) and SHOW AND TELL (Page 86) upon the completion and approval of the student's written report.

Note: During a science fair, things get moved around. It is easy for things to get misplaced. You can avoid this by having your students fill out the science project identification forms: SCIENCE PROJECT IDENTIFICATION (Page 89), and SCIENCE PROJECT IDENTIFICATION TAGS (Page 90).

Tape or attach a SCIENCE PROJECT IDENTIFICATION form to the back of each project display board. The form contains a place for a photograph of the completed display, to assist those in charge of transporting the project (if it is not the student) in its reassembly.

Use the SCIENCE PROJECT IDENTIFICATION TAGS to match up the board with the box(es) containing the materials for the front of the display. The small tags may be attached to the bottoms of any loose items as an added precaution.

Also, during the time a science project is on display, elements of it may be affected by handling, or from lack of maintenance — e.g., watering of plants, leaking containers, disarrangement of the display by curious viewers, etc.

The MAINTENANCE AGREEMENT (Page 91) form can be filled out and attached to the board, and a copy kept with the teacher or science fair coordinator. The agreement identifies the elements of the display that may need periodic upkeep or checking, as well as designates the person who will be responsible for doing this.

OBJECTIVE: EVALUATE THE SCIENCE FAIR EXPERIENCE.

It is important that each child evaluate his or her science fair experience.

Use MY SCIENCE PROJECT EVALUATION (Page 92) for the evaluation form. Have parents return the PARENT'S EVALUATION distributed earlier.

ALSO:

At the end of this book are several pages of blank grids. Students may use them to construct charts, graphs, or design their display boards.

A LETTER TO PARENTS

Our ability to solve present and future problems depends on our ability to question the world in new and creative ways. With our knowledge of the world growing so rapidly, we must move away from having our children simply memorize facts. Computers can do that much better and more efficiently. Instead, we must emphasize the **thinking skills** that can put those facts to use, and create organization for new facts as they emerge.

What better opportunity for a child to develop such skills than to participate in his or her school's science fair! The thinking skills a child develops while doing a science fair project are the same basic skills he or she will use daily throughout his or her life — to sense and clarify problems that exist, and to find creative solutions to those problems.

Please encourage your child to take part in this year's science fair. Children should select projects that match their interests and abilities. The science fair experience should be FUN for your child — something he or she really wants to do.

The Science Fair Comic Book, an informative comic book-style story your child will be bringing home shortly, summarizes the steps to planning, completing, and presenting a science fair project. By reading *The Science Fair Comic Book* along with your child, you will help to reinforce the concepts being taught in the classroom. And, you will perhaps be better able to answer your child's questions about his or her science fair project.

Sincerely,

The Science Fair Committee

DO'S AND DON'TS

Very often parents think that winning an award is the goal of a science fair competition. But, EVERY child who participates in a science fair is a winner. Here are some suggestions for helping your child "win" with his or her science project.

DO'S

DO ENCOURAGE participation in the SCIENCE FAIR at your child's school.

DO ASK to see the science project-related worksheets your child does at school. Help your child fill out homework assignments the teacher gives him/her. If you need to, have your child dictate what he/she wants to say. Except for spelling and grammatical corrections, avoid putting your words into your child's mouth.

DO OFFER to take your child to libraries, museums, or other places where he/she may get information during the research phase of the investigation. You can also help your child contact people who may be able to provide information about his/her topic.

DO HELP your child acquire the materials needed for the project.

DO LISTEN if your child wants to talk through his/her ideas. Communicate to your child the message, "I'm interested in what you are doing." Give honest feedback, but do so in a positive way. You never want to diminish a child's efforts. You always want the child to know you are **proud** of his/her efforts — especially when the child wants to "figure it out" by himself/herself.

DO READ *The Science Fair Comic Book* with your child.

DO HAVE your child take necessary safety precautions. Do not let him/her do anything that may be dangerous.

DO HELP your child construct a realistic time frame for completion.

DO OFFER assistance in transporting project materials to and from school.

DO CONTACT your child's teacher if you have any questions regarding procedures.

DON'TS

DON'T DO the work for your child. Remember that this is your **child's** science project, not **yours**. Doing your child's project for him/her is like telling him/her, "I don't want you to think for yourself." Give your child room to make mistakes. That's the only way he/she will learn. If the project seems too hard, then the child should select one that can be handled. It does little good to "bail" a child out of too ambitious a project by doing it for him/her.

DON'T ENCOURAGE your child to do a "canned" science demonstration from a book. Demonstrations **can** be used to illustrate a principle **related to** the investigation. But, it should not **be** the investigation itself.

DON'T MAKE the focus of the project a competition — the "winning" — at a science fair. It's nice to get a ribbon, but the purpose of the fair is for the child to exercise thinking skills and to expand his/her knowledge of a topic area. This makes EVERY child a winner!

SCIENCE PROJECT COMPLETION SCHEDULE

for _____

Keep this schedule in a place where it is easily seen.

ASSIGNMENT	Date Due	Date Completed
Question		
Hypothesis		
Project Proposal		
Journal		
Report		
Project Display		
Oral Presentation		
Evaluation		

PARENT'S EVALUATION

Name of child participating in the SCIENCE FAIR: _____

Name(s) of parent(s) observing child's participation in the SCIENCE FAIR:

_____

_____

Was this year's SCIENCE FAIR a good experience for your child? _____

Explain. _____

_____

_____

Was this year's SCIENCE FAIR a good experience for you? _____

Explain. _____

_____

_____

What did you feel your child learned from doing his or her project? _____

_____

_____

What did you learn about your child from watching him or her do this project? _____

_____

_____

Do you think your child was prepared to do this project? _____

Explain. _____

_____

Do you have any suggestions for improvement? _____

_____

_____

_____

_____

_____   _____
Signature   Date

_____   _____
Signature   Date

After the SCIENCE FAIR is over, please
return this form to your child's teacher.

The SCIENCE FAIR Comic Book

by John and
Patty Carratello

Illustrated by
Anna Chellton

This comic book belongs to _____

Teacher _____

School _____

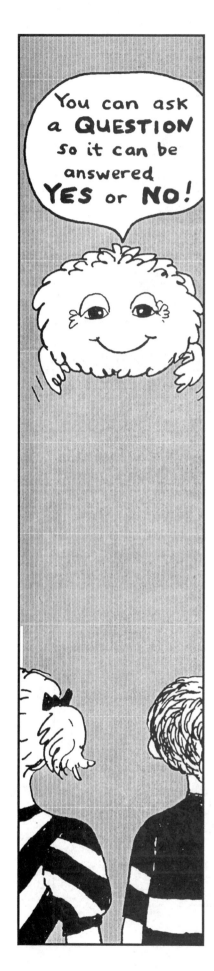

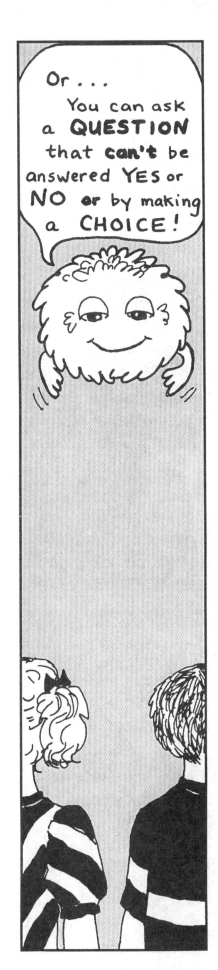

That's, okay. Figuring out ahead of time what materials you will need for your project takes **PRACTICE!**

And, so does writing good **STEP-BY-STEP DIRECTIONS!**

Directions for **WHAT?**

Directions for your **PROCEDURE!**

There are a lot of things in your testing that you need to keep the same, or **CONTROL** so the testing is **FAIR!**

If you don't plan out what you are going to measure and how you are going to measure it **BEFORE** you actually do it, things may happen that can spoil your investigation.

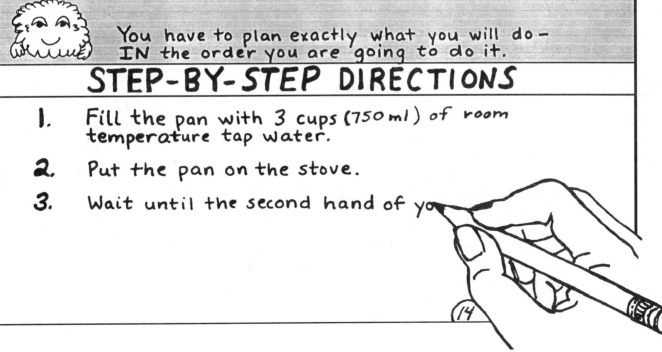

You have to plan exactly what you will do— IN the order you are going to do it.

STEP-BY-STEP DIRECTIONS

1. Fill the pan with 3 cups (750 ml) of room temperature tap water.

2. Put the pan on the stove.

3. Wait until the second hand of yo

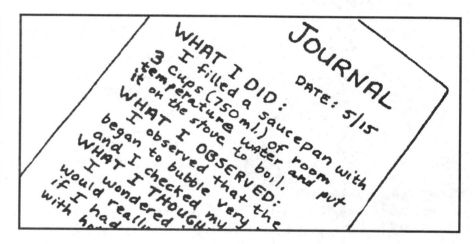

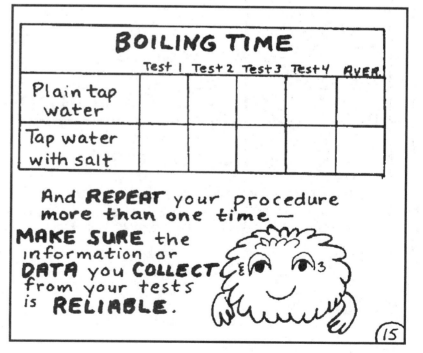

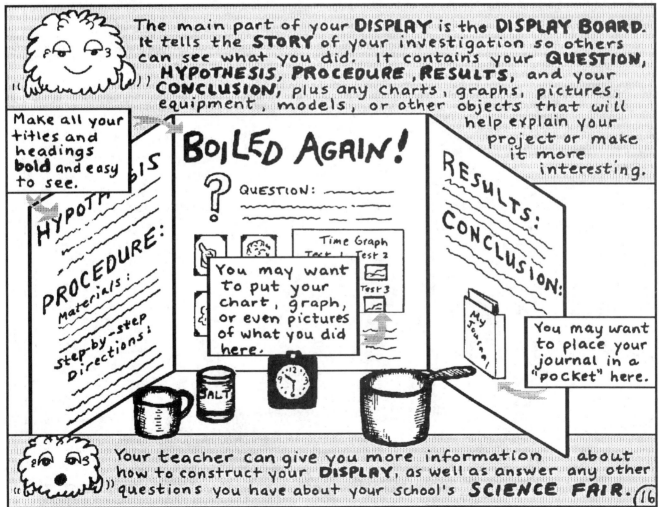

SCIENCE PROJECT
CHECKLIST

☐ Ask a QUESTION that you can investigate yourself.

☐ Begin a JOURNAL to write down everything you do, observe, and think during your investigation.

☐ Do RESEARCH on the TOPIC of your question.

☐ Form a HYPOTHESIS about what you *think* the answer to your question will be.

☐ Plan a PROCEDURE to TEST your hypothesis. Decide what MATERIALS you will need and write STEP-BY-STEP DIRECTIONS for what you will do and how you will do it. Make sure you follow the rules for SCIENCE SAFETY and WORKING WITH ANIMALS.

☐ Construct a CHART to help you COLLECT and ORGANIZE your DATA.

☐ Fill our your SCIENCE PROJECT PROPOSAL and sign it. Then, have your teacher and your parents sign it too! Do this *before* you actually do the steps of your procedure.

☐ Follow the step-by-step directions of your procedure and RECORD your data onto your chart.

☐ Summarize the RESULTS of your testing in a WRITTEN SUMMARY.

☐ Make a GRAPH of the results, so others can see *at a glance* what you've learned.

☐ Write a CONCLUSION statement which either restates your hypothesis (if it is supported) or revises it (if it is not supported).

☐ Write a SCIENCE PROJECT REPORT that summarizes your investigation.

☐ Be prepared to give an ORAL PRESENTATION.

☐ Construct your SCIENCE PROJECT DISPLAY.

☐ Complete your SCIENCE PROJECT EVALUATION.

THINGS I WOULD LIKE TO KNOW
MORE
ABOUT!

☐ **Check the things that you are curious about.**

☐ What makes a rainbow?   ☐ How do plants grow?
☐ How does sound travel?   ☐ Why does a ball bounce?
☐ Why does a dog pant?   ☐ What makes soap clean?
☐ What makes some rocks smooth? ☐ Why do leaves change color?
☐ How do scissors work?   ☐ What makes water boil?

Write some of your own ideas here.

☐ _____
☐ _____
☐ _____

☐ **Check the subjects that you would like to know more about.**

☐ mirrors	☐ my body	☐ sound
☐ plants	☐ heat	☐ wind
☐ magic	☐ kites	☐ prisms
☐ radios	☐ air	☐ gravity
☐ light	☐ baseball	☐ batteries
☐ coins	☐ animals	☐ seeing
☐ water	☐ paper airplanes	☐ hearing
☐ soap	☐ magnets	☐ tasting
☐ electricity	☐ shells	☐ touching
☐ bicycles	☐ fire	☐ smelling

Write some of your own ideas here.

☐ _____   ☐ _____
☐ _____   ☐ _____
☐ _____   ☐ _____

MANY WAYS TO ASK!

There are several ways to ask a question.

1. You can ask a question that can be answered "yes" or "no."

2. You can ask a question that can be answered by making a choice.

3. You can ask a question that can't be answered "yes" or "no" or by making a choice.

Here are ten questions. <u>Underline</u> the questions that can be answered by a "yes" or a "no." Circle the questions that can be answered by making a choice. Put a box around the question that can't be answered by a "yes" or "no," or by making a choice.

1. Does anyone in my class have the same fingerprints?

2. Which brand of soap makes the most suds?

3. How many seeds does an apple have?

4. In which type of water do plants grow best?

5. Can you tell where sound comes from when you are blindfolded?

6. Which brand of paper towel absorbs the most water?

7. How much salt does it take to float an egg?

8. Does the color of water affect its evaporation?

9. Does a plant need oxygen?

10. Which metal conducts heat best?

CAN I DO IT MYSELF?

When you ask a question for a science project, you have to be sure you can answer it all by yourself, without finding the answer in a book or by asking someone else.

Put a check mark next to the questions you would be able to find the answer to by yourself.

_____ 1. What is the temperature on Venus?

_____ 2. How does a tree grow?

_____ 3. How many raisins are in the most popular brands of cereal?

_____ 4. When can I find the most worms in my backyard?

_____ 5. What types of plants grow best in shade?

_____ 6. How do airplanes fly?

_____ 7. What is the fastest animal in the world?

_____ 8. Does air exert pressure?

_____ 9. How much can a caterpillar eat in one day?

_____ 10. How big is the moon?

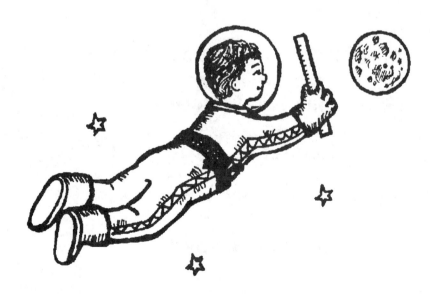

I HAVE QUESTIONS about things I've seen people do around my house.

? For example . . . I saw my father cover a pot of water with a lid before putting it on the stove. **I wonder** — Does water boil faster with a lid or without a lid? ?

One thing I saw someone do around my house was _____

_____

_____ .

I wonder — _____

_____

_____

_____ ?

Another thing I saw someone do around my house was _____

_____

_____ .

I wonder — _____

_____

_____

_____ ?

I HAVE QUESTIONS about things I've read.

? ? For example . . . I read that cheetahs run 70 ? ?
miles per hour (110 kilometers per hour). **I**
? **wonder** — Can anyone in my class run that ?
? fast?

One thing I read
was _____
_____
_____
_____
_____
_____
_____ .

I wonder —_____
_____
_____
_____
_____
_____
_____
_____ ?

Another thing I
read was _____
_____
_____
_____
_____
_____
_____ .

I wonder —_____
_____
_____
_____
_____
_____
_____
_____ ?

I HAVE QUESTIONS about things I've seen and heard on television.

? ? ?

For example . . . I saw a bowl filled with strawberries and covered with plastic food wrap turned upside down — and the strawberries stayed in the bowl! **I wonder** — Can a bowl covered with plastic food wrap be turned upside down without spilling what is inside?

? ? ?

One thing I saw or heard on T.V. was

_____

_____

_____ .

I wonder — _____

_____

_____

_____ ?

Another thing I saw or heard on T.V. was

_____

_____

_____ .

I wonder — _____

_____

_____

_____ ?

I HAVE QUESTIONS about things I've thought about all by myself.

? **?** **?** **?** **?** **?**

For example . . . I saw many ants covering a piece of cookie that had been dropped on the playground. **I wonder** — What kind of food from my lunch will ants like best?

One thing I thought was _____
_____
_____
_____ .

I wonder — _____
_____
_____
_____ ?

Another thing I thought was _____
_____
_____
_____ .

I wonder — _____
_____
_____
_____
_____ ?

NARROW IT DOWN!

Choose two of your favorite questions from **your questions** that the teacher has already seen. Neatly write them here.

Question 1: _____

_____

_____

_____

_____

_____

Question 2: _____

_____

_____

_____

_____

_____

#228 All About Science Fairs

MY BEST QUESTION!

With which one of your questions can you do the best job? Fill in the following information, then make your decision.

You will want to select the question that can be investigated with materials you have or can get. You will also want to select a question for which you have enough resources to find out about your subject.

Question 1

Materials I have or can get:

_____

_____

_____

Resources (books, magazines, people, etc.) I have to find out more about my subject:

_____

_____

_____

Question 2

Materials I have or can get:

_____

_____

_____

Resources (books, magazines, people, etc.) I have to find out more about my subject:

_____

_____

_____

After thinking about the materials and resources I have listed above, I feel the best question to use for my project is Question # _____.

MAKE IT CLEAR!

When your science project question is clearly written, the project is much easier to do. That is because the question itself tells you what you will need to measure.

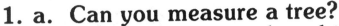

Circle the letter of the question that is asked more clearly.

1. a. Can you measure a tree?
   b. Can you estimate how high a tree is by measuring its shadow?

2. a. Which type of orange has the most juice?
   b. Are oranges juicy?

3. a. Which brand of battery lasts longer?
   b. Which brand of battery is best?

4. a. Are mice smart?
   b. Can a mouse find food in a maze?

5. a. Will bean seeds germinate in a liquid other than water?
   b. How do bean seeds grow?

6. a. Does a ball roll faster on grass or dirt?
   b. How fast can a ball roll?

7. a. Does a plant grow better in sunlight or in artificial light?
   b. How do plants grow?

SCIENCE PROJECT IDEAS - LEVEL 1

1.	How much salt does it take to float an egg?	21.	Do bigger seeds produce bigger plants?
2.	What kind of juice cleans pennies best?	22.	Which materials absorb the most water?
3.	Which dish soap makes the most bubbles?	23.	Do wheels reduce friction?
4.	Do watches keep time the same?	24.	What materials dissolve in water?
5.	On which surface can a snail move faster — dirt or cement?	25.	What is the soil in my schoolyard made of?
6.	What brand of raisin cereal has the most raisins?	26.	Does holding a mirror in front of a fish change what a fish does?
7.	How can you measure the strength of a magnet?	27.	What color of birdseed do birds like best?
8.	Do ants like cheese or sugar better?	28.	What holds two boards together better — a nail or a screw?
9.	Can the design of a paper airplane make it fly farther?	29.	Will bananas brown faster on the counter or in the refrigerator?
10.	Do roots of a plant always grow downward?	30.	Does temperature affect the growth of plants?
11.	Can you tell what something is just by touching it?	31.	Do mint leaves repel ants?
12.	What kind of things do magnets attract?	32.	Does a ball roll farther on grass or dirt?
13.	What foods do mealworms prefer?	33.	Do all objects fall to the ground at the same speed?
14.	How long will it take a drop of food dye to color a glass of still water?	34.	Does anyone in my class have the same fingerprints?
15.	Does a bath take less water than a shower?	35.	Which travels faster — a snail or a worm?
16.	Can you tell where sound comes from when you are blindfolded?	36.	Which paper towel is the strongest?
17.	Can plants grow without soil?	37.	Can plants grow from leaves?
18.	Does warm water freeze faster than cool water?	38.	Which dissolves better in water — salt or baking soda?
19.	In my class who is taller — boys or girls?	39.	Can things be identified by just their smell?
20.	Do different types of apples have the same number of seeds?	40.	With which type of battery do toys run longest?

SCIENCE PROJECT IDEAS - LEVEL 2

1.	How far does a snail travel in one minute?	21.	Does the color of water affect its evaporation?
2.	Do different types of soil hold different amounts of water?	22.	Can you separate salt from water by freezing?
3.	Will adding bleach to the water of a plant reduce fungus growth?	23.	How does omitting an ingredient affect the taste of a cookie?
4.	Does water with salt boil faster than plain water?	24.	Do suction cups stick equally well to different surfaces?
5.	How far can a person lean without falling?	25.	Which student in class has the greatest lung capacity?
6.	Can you tell time without a watch or clock?	26.	How much weight can a growing plant lift?
7.	How far can a water balloon be tossed to someone before it breaks?	27.	Will water with salt evaporate faster than water without salt?
8.	Does the shape of a kite affect its flight?	28.	Does it matter in which direction seeds are planted?
9.	Does an ice cube melt faster in air or water?	29.	Which cheese grows mold the fastest?
10.	Does sugar prolong the life of cut flowers?	30.	Do all colors fade at the same rate?
11.	How much of an orange is water?	31.	Which brand of diaper holds the most water?
12.	Which liquid has the highest viscosity?	32.	In my class, who has the smallest hands — boys or girls?
13.	Will more air inside a basketball make it bounce higher?	33.	Which kind of cleaner removes ink stains best?
14.	Does the color of light affect plant growth?	34.	Does a plant grow bigger if watered by milk or water?
15.	Does baking soda lower the temperature of water?	35.	Which brand of soap makes the most suds?
16.	Which brand of popcorn pops the most kernels?	36.	Does a baseball go farther when hit by a wood or metal bat?
17.	Which brand of popcorn pops the fastest?	37.	Do living plants give off moisture?
18.	How much can a caterpillar eat in one day?	38.	Using a lever, can one student lift another student who is bigger?
19.	In my class, who has the biggest feet — boys or girls?	39.	What gets warmer — sand or dirt?
20.	Do plants grow bigger in soil or water?	40.	Which kind of glue holds two boards together better?

SCIENCE PROJECT IDEAS - LEVEL 3

1. What type of line carries sound waves best?
2. Can the sun's energy be used to clean water?
3. Does a green plant add oxygen to its environment?
4. Which metal conducts heat best?
5. What percentage of corn seeds in a package will germinate?
6. Does an earthworm react to light and darkness?
7. Does the human tongue have definite areas for certain tastes?
8. Can same-type balloons withstand the same amount of pressure?
9. Does the viscosity of a liquid affect its boiling point?
10. Does surrounding color affect an insect's eating habits?
11. Do children's heart rates increase as they get older?
12. Can you use a strand of human hair to measure air moisture?
13. What materials provide the best insulation?
14. Is using two eyes to judge distance more accurate than using one eye?
15. Do different kinds of caterpillars eat different amounts of food?
16. What plant foods contain starch?
17. What keeps things colder — plastic wrap or aluminum foil?
18. Does heart rate increase with increasing sound volume?
19. Do boys or girls have a higher resting heart rate?
20. Do liquids cool as they evaporate?
21. Which way does the wind blow most frequently?
22. Does the size of a light bulb affect its energy use?
23. For how long a distance can speech be transmitted through a tube?
24. Which grows mold faster — moist bread or dry bread?
25. What type of soil filters water best?
26. Does the color of a material affect its absorption of heat?
27. Does sound travel best through solids, liquids, or gases?
28. Do sugar crystals grow faster in tap water or distilled water?
29. Can you see better if you limit the light that gets to your eye?
30. How much of an apple is water?
31. What common liquids are acid, base, or neutral?
32. Do taller people run faster than shorter people?
33. Does the length of a vibrating object affect sound?
34. Does a plant need some darkness to grow?
35. Who can balance better on the balls of their feet — boys or girls?
36. Does exercise affect heart rate?
37. Which dish soap makes the longest lasting suds?
38. What are the effects of chlorine on plant growth?
39. Which type of oil has the greatest density?
40. How accurately do people judge temperatures?

POLISHING MY QUESTION!

Write your project question here.

_____

_____

_____

_____

_____

_____

Ask someone to check your question. Write down any suggestions this person has to make your question more clear.

_____

_____

_____

_____

_____

Use these suggestions to help make your question as clear as possible. Write your polished question here.

_____

_____

_____

_____

_____

_____

_____

_____

_____

MY QUESTION!

Write the question you have chosen for your science project inside the question mark.

Write your name inside the circle.

Dear Diary . . .

A scientific JOURNAL is like a diary. In a diary, you write down everything you do, observe, and think about each day.

For one day, write down things you did, observed, and thought about. You may ask someone to help you record what you want to say.

DATE: _____

WHAT I DID: _____
_____
_____
_____
_____
_____

WHAT I OBSERVED: _____
_____
_____
_____
_____
_____

WHAT I THOUGHT: _____
_____
_____
_____
_____
_____
_____

55

MY JOURNAL

Date started _____

Date ended _____

My Journal — Research Entry   DATE: _____

SOURCE OF INFORMATION:

_____

_____

_____

_____

_____

_____

WHAT I FOUND OUT:

_____

_____

_____

_____

_____

_____

_____

_____

_____

_____

_____

_____

_____

_____

_____

_____

_____

My Journal — Test Entry

DATE: _____

WHAT I DID: _____
_____
_____
_____
_____
_____
_____
_____
_____

WHAT I OBSERVED:

Time Observation Began

Time Observation Ended

a.m. ____:____
p.m.

a.m. ____:____
p.m.

_____
_____
_____
_____

WHAT I THOUGHT:
_____
_____
_____
_____
_____
_____

My Journal — General Entry

inventions

charts

ideas

doodles

thoughts

photos

drawings

pictures

WHAT NEXT?

Each of these pictures can have several different things happen because of the action in each picture. Cut *hypothesis ideas* from the idea page. Paste your ideas under each picture. Do not use the ideas that could not *really* happen.

Paste hypothesis idea here.	Paste hypothesis idea here.	Paste hypothesis idea here.
Paste hypothesis idea here.	Paste hypothesis idea here.	Paste hypothesis idea here.
Paste hypothesis idea here.	Paste hypothesis idea here.	Paste hypothesis idea here.

#228 All About Science Fairs

IDEA PAGE FOR "WHAT NEXT?"

Cut these pictures out. Use these ideas for making your "WHAT NEXT?" page.

WHAT WAS THE QUESTION?

When you form your hypothesis, it must match your question.

Circle the letter you think was the question for each hypothesis given.

1. HYPOTHESIS: Water will boil faster on a gas burner.

a. How fast can water boil?
b. Will water boil faster on a gas burner or on an electric burner?
c. Will water boil fast when it is put on a gas burner?

2. HYPOTHESIS: People can tell the difference between an apple and a pear when they are blindfolded.

a. What type of fruit do people prefer — apples or pears?
b. How can people tell the difference between an apple and a pear?
c. Can people tell the difference between an apple and a pear when they are blindfolded?

3. HYPOTHESIS: Living plants give off water.

a. Do living plants give off water?
b. How much water does a living plant give off?
c. Which type of plants give off the most water — living plants or freshly cut plants?

4. HYPOTHESIS: A person can lean twelve inches without falling.

a. How far can people lean?
b. How far can a person lean without falling?
c. How long does it take before a person falls over?

I PREDICT!

Write a hypothesis for each question. Make believe you have already done your research. The purpose of this worksheet isn't for you to get the right answer. The purpose is to write a good hypothesis.

1. How many days will it take a potato to sprout?

   _____

   _____

   _____

2. What is the average number of raisins in a box of Really Raisins breakfast cereal?

   _____

   _____

   _____

   _____

3. Which dissolves more completely in water — salt or baking soda?

   _____

   _____

   _____

4. How many seeds does a Washington apple have?

   _____

   _____

   _____

   _____

I THINK . . .

Write the question you have chosen for your project.

_____

_____

_____

_____

_____

Next, write your hypothesis. Then have your teacher read it and make suggestions for improvement.

_____

_____

_____

_____

_____

Now, write your hypothesis **again**. Fix anything that needs improvement.

_____

_____

_____

_____

_____

_____

MATERIALS LIST

List the exact materials you will need to complete your project in the left-hand column. When you are finished, you and your teacher will circle the items that could be more clear. Then, in the right-hand column, list your clearly-defined materials.

Example: battery —————————————→ D-cell battery
          (unclear)   (clear)

My Materials

_____
_____
_____
_____
_____
_____
_____
_____
_____
_____
_____
_____
_____
_____
_____
_____
_____
_____
_____
_____

My Materials Revised

_____
_____
_____
_____
_____
_____
_____
_____
_____
_____
_____
_____
_____
_____
_____
_____
_____
_____
_____
_____

CONTROL!

When testing your hypothesis, you must make sure that your test is a FAIR TEST! To do so, you must CONTROL all the varibles in your test, except for the one variable you will change (manipulate) to test your hypothesis. Scientists call the things that need to be kept the same the *controlled variables*. They call the one thing that is changed the *manipulated variable*.

Here are two hypotheses. Below each one, list the variable that will need to be changed (manipulated) so you may test the hypothesis, as well as the variables that will need to be kept the same (controlled) in order to make the test fair.

HYPOTHESIS 1: Rapid-Pop Popcorn will pop more kernels than Puffy Popcorn.

The one variable I will need to change (manipulate) so I may test this hypothesis is:

_____

The variables I will need to keep the same (control) to make this a fair test are:

_____

_____

HYPOTHESIS 2: People can lean between 6 and 12 inches (15 and 30 centimeters) forward before they begin to fall.

The one variable I will need to change (manipulate) so I may test this hypothesis is:

_____

The variables I will need to keep the same (control) to make this a fair test are:

_____

_____

_____

ORDER!

Drawn on this page are four steps in a procedure for a science investigation that compares leading dish soaps in their ability to make bubbles. Cut out each picture. Then, arrange the pictures in a logical, step-by-step order.

"THE WINNER"

PEANUT BUTTER AND JELLY

Work in a group of 3 or 4.
Explain how to make a peanut butter and jelly sandwich.

Step-By-Step Directions:
(Number each of your steps.)

_____

_____

_____

_____

_____

_____

_____

_____

PEANUT BUTTER

JELLY

Exchange your papers with another group. Can you follow each other's directions? Try it!

TESTING: 1, 2, 3 . . .

Write your hypothesis.

_____

_____

_____

Below, write the steps you will take to test your hypothesis. Skip a line between each step, in case you want to add something later. Be as clear as you can with your directions. Someone else should be able to follow your steps. When you are finished, go back and number your steps.

_____

_____

_____

_____

_____

_____

_____

_____

_____

_____

_____

_____

_____

_____

_____

_____

_____

SCIENCE SAFETY

Are you a safe scientist? Read these safety rules and **REMEMBER** them. The rules listed below will help protect you and others.

1. Wash your hands thoroughly before and after an experiment.

2. Protect your clothing by wearing an old T-shirt, and protect the surface of the desk or table you are working on by covering it with newspapers.

3. Keep long hair and loose clothing out of the way while doing an investigation.

4. Know the location of the first aid kit, fire alarm, fire extinguisher, and nurse. Use safety equipment if needed.

5. Find out if your teacher has any special rules about safety for fire, electricity, animals, chemical use, or anything else.

6. Smother fires by using something like a towel or sweater. If your clothing does catch fire, smother it or STOP, DROP, and ROLL. *NEVER RUN!*

7. Take out an electrical plug from an outlet by pulling the plug instead of the cord.

8. Make sure all investigations using living things are approved.

9. Handle chemicals only under the supervision of an adult.

10. Follow directions carefully. If you don't know what to do, ask for help.

11. Report any accidents to your teacher.

12. Do not bump into others.

13. Clean up carefully after every science activity. Return all materials to the places they belong.

14. Stay alert and careful!

WORKING WITH ANIMALS

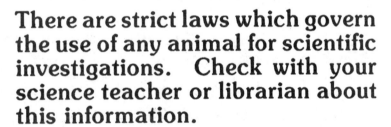

Animals are often used in scientific investigations. They have helped us discover many important things. However, when we use animals for scientific reasons, we must remember to be careful with them. Animals are **LIVING THINGS**, and we should treat them with respect.

There are strict laws which govern the use of any animal for scientific investigations. Check with your science teacher or librarian about this information.

REMEMBER — If you are using an animal in your investigation — **BE CARING!**

MAKE A RECORD

As you carry out the procedure of your investigation, you need a way to collect and organize the data (measurements) you get — a way to write them down, or record them. A good way is to make up a chart.

Make up a chart for the types of data you would expect to collect while investigating the question below. Use the grid to help you plan out and draw your chart. Then, do the investigation to answer the question. Use your chart to record your data.

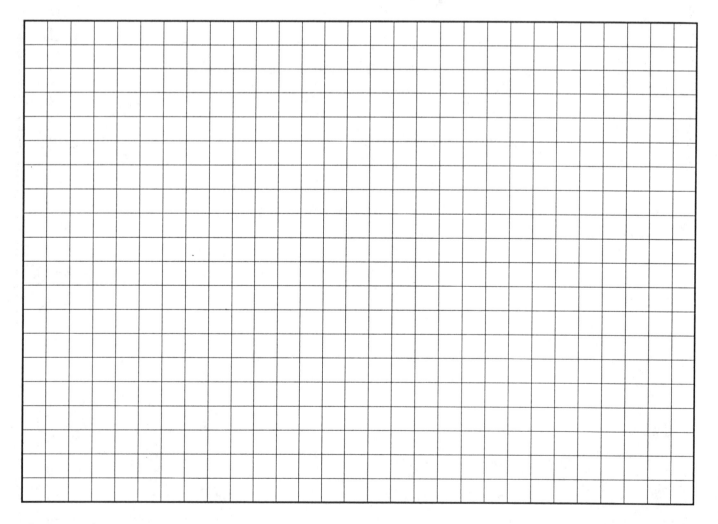

QUESTION: How far can a water balloon be tossed to someone before it breaks?

JUST AVERAGE

Make believe you are doing the following science investigation.

Your QUESTION is:
How many raisins are there in a box of Really Raisins Cereal?

Your HYPOTHESIS is:
There are between 50 and 60 raisins in a box of Really Raisins Cereal.

Your PROCEDURE (the measuring part) is to:
Count the number of raisins in three same-size boxes of Really Raisins Cereal.

Fill in the number of raisins you will find in each box.

TEST #1
Raisin Count

_____

TEST #2
Raisin Count

_____

TEST #3
Raisin Count

_____

Now, show how you will average all 3 raisin counts to come up with a SINGLE final raisin count.

TEST #1 _____

TEST #2 _____

TEST #3 _____

TOTAL _____

(Divide by 3)

AVERAGE _____

I PROPOSE

the following investigation for my

SCIENCE FAIR PROJECT

Project Title: _____

QUESTION (What I want to find out.)

_____
_____
_____

HYPOTHESIS (What I think will be the answer to my
question.)

_____
_____
_____

PROCEDURE (How I will test my hypothesis.)
Materials Needed: _____

_____
_____

Step-By-Step Directions: (Number each step.)

_____
_____
_____
_____
_____
_____
_____
_____
_____
_____

Step-By-Step Directions: (Cont.)

_____

_____

_____

_____

_____

_____

_____

_____

_____

_____

_____

_____

_____

_____

_____

_____

This is the investigation I would like to do for my SCIENCE FAIR PROJECT.

_____   _____
Student's Signature   Date

The investigation outlined in this proposal meets the preliminary requirements for a SCIENCE FAIR PROJECT.

_____   _____
Teacher's Signature   Date

I will support my child's efforts in doing this SCIENCE FAIR PROJECT.

_____   _____
Parent's Signature   Date

PUT IT IN WRITING!

The following chart contains the data collected in an investigation in which someone wanted to know, in comparing the three leading brands of raisin cereal, "Which brand of raisin cereal has the most raisins?"

RAISIN COUNT — BRAND A

Test 1	Test 2	Test 3	Test 4	AVERAGE
120	115	122	127	121

RAISIN COUNT — BRAND B

Test 1	Test 2	Test 3	Test 4	AVERAGE
138	141	132	137	137

RAISIN COUNT — BRAND C

Test 1	Test 2	Test 3	Test 4	AVERAGE
129	119	123	129	125

Below, fill in the results of the person's investigation.

RESULTS

The average number of raisins in a box of BRAND A cereal was _____.

The average number of raisins in a box of BRAND B cereal was _____.

The average number of raisins in a box of BRAND C cereal was _____.

READ A LINE GRAPH

Jason's science project question is, "Does the temperature on the playground increase more under the big willow tree, or by the swing during the day?" He collected data each day for a week, and averaged his results. Then, to more easily see the results, he made a *LINE GRAPH*.

Use the graph to answer the questions below.

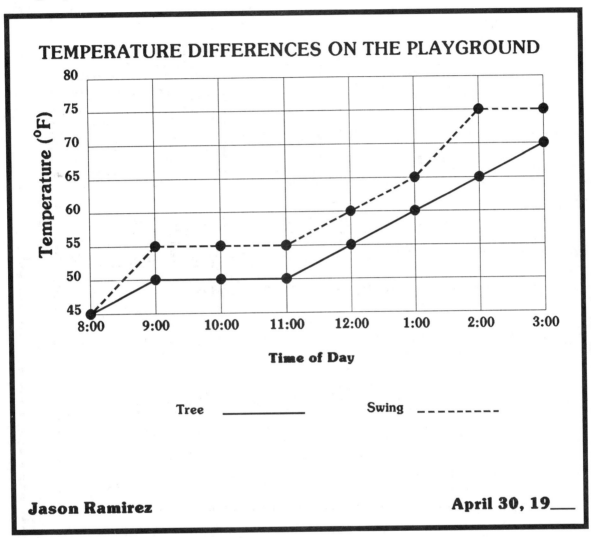

1. What is the graph about? _____

2. What was measured? _____

3. When were the measurements taken? _____

4. How much did the temperature increase from 8:00 to 3:00 under the tree? _____ How much did the temperature increase during the same time by the swing? _____

5. Does Jason's graph provide the information he needs to answer his question? _____

MAKE A LINE GRAPH

Kary's science project question is, "What is the warmest time of the day at school, during the month of March?" She collected her data each day for an entire month, then made a chart to show the average temperature for each time of the day students are at school. However, she also wants to show the results of her investigation on a *LINE GRAPH*.

Use the data on the chart to complete Kary's graph. Be sure you label both the vertical and horizontal sides of the graph, plot the data points, then connect them.

Time of Day	8:00	9:00	10:00	11:00	12:00	1:00	2:00	3:00
Average Temperature (Degrees Fahrenheit)	50	51	53	54	55	57	58	58

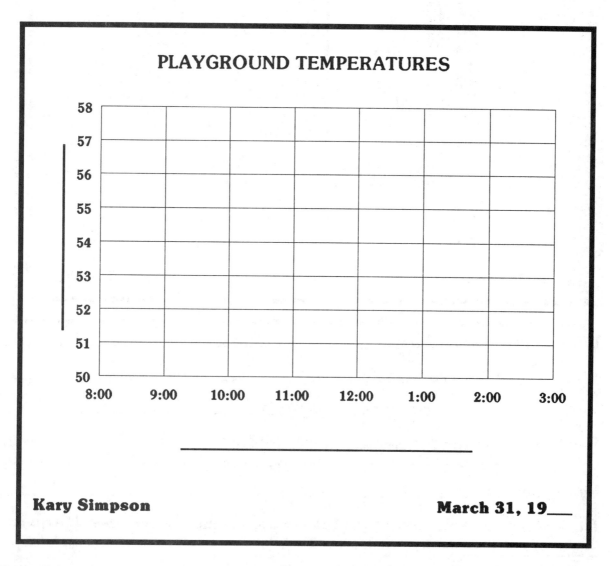

PLAYGROUND TEMPERATURES

Kary Simpson   March 31, 19___

READ A BAR GRAPH

Herlinda's science project question is, "Who uses the most water for baths and showers at my house?" She showed her family how to take the measurements she needed, which they did for a week. Then, after averaging the data, she made a *BAR GRAPH* to more easily see the results.

Use the graph to answer the questions below.

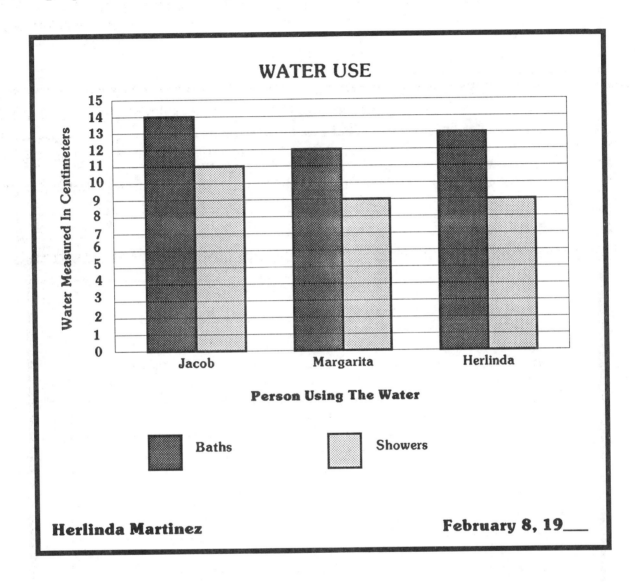

1. What is the graph about? _____

2. What is being compared? _____

3. How much more water does Jacob use for baths than Herlinda? _____

4. Who used the same amount of water for their showers? _____

5. Does Herlinda's graph provide the information she needs to answer her question? _____

MAKE A BAR GRAPH

Karl's science project question is, "Do the people in my house use more water when they take baths, or when they take showers?" After showing the people in his family how to take the measurements he needed, he collected the data and made a chart to show the results of each test. When he was done, he decided he would also like to more easily show the results of his investigation by making a *BAR GRAPH* showing the total averages.

Use the data on the chart to complete Karl's graph. Be sure to label both the vertical and horizontal sides of the graph. Then plan out the length, width, and spacing of the bars on the grid, before filling them in.

WATER USED FOR BATHS AND SHOWERS
(Measured In Centimeters)

	TEST 1		TEST 2		TEST 3		TEST 4		Bath Average	Shower Average
	Bath	Shower	Bath	Shower	Bath	Shower	Bath	Shower		
Mark	14	10	12	12	14	12	16	10	14	11
Karl	10	9	14	9	12	10	12	8	12	9
Kamila	15	10	12	9	12	8	13	9	13	9
							TOTAL Averages		13	10

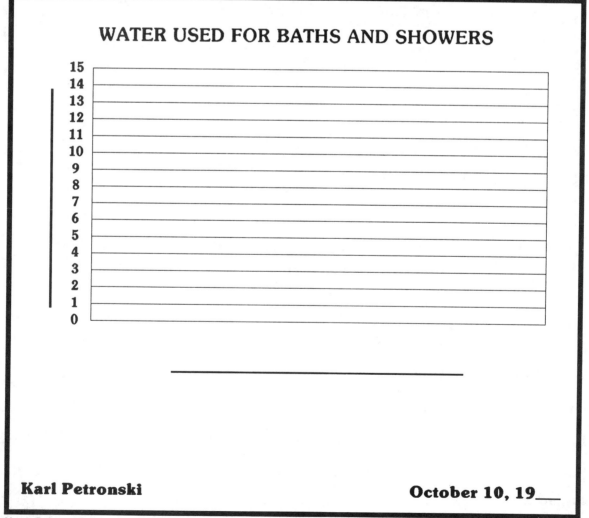

WATER USED FOR BATHS AND SHOWERS

Karl Petronski   **October 10, 19___**

IN CONCLUSION . . .

Complete the conclusion statement for each of the following projects. To do so, first carefully read the hypothesis. Then pay close attention to the results. Be sure your conclusion statement reflects your results.

PROJECT 1

HYPOTHESIS: People use more water when they take a bath than when they take a shower.

RESULTS: The water used for baths averaged 6 inches (15 centimeters) deep.

The water used for showers averaged 4 inches (10 centimeters) deep.

CONCLUSION: The results show my hypothesis is _____ (supported or not supported). People use more water when they take a _____ than when they take a _____.

PROJECT 2

HYPOTHESIS: Aspirin will prolong the life of cut flowers.

RESULTS: The cut flowers placed in water without aspirin began to wither in 5 days.

The cut flowers placed in water with aspirin began to wither in 8 days.

CONCLUSION: The results show my hypothesis is _____ (supported or not supported). Aspirin _____ (does or does not) prolong the life of cut flowers.

PROJECT TITLE:

_____

_____

_____

Question

_____
_____

Hypothesis

_____
_____

Procedure

Materials Needed:

_____
_____
_____
_____
_____

Step-By-Step Directions: (Please number each step.)

_____
_____
_____
_____
_____
_____
_____
_____
_____

_____

_____

_____

_____

_____

_____

_____

_____

_____

_____

_____

Results

_____

_____

_____

_____

_____

_____

Conclusion

_____

_____

_____

_____

_____

_____

APPROVED:

_____   _____
      Teacher   **Date**

SAVE THIS REPORT!
All the information that is contained in this report will go on your SCIENCE PROJECT DISPLAY BOARD.

MY ORAL PRESENTATION

Use the following outline as a guide.

My name is _____.

I am in the _____ grade at _____ School.

The title of my project is _____.

I became interested in doing this project when _____

_____.

The QUESTION I asked was _____

_____.

The HYPOTHESIS I formed was _____

_____.

The PROCEDURE I used to test my hypothesis was to _____

_____

_____

_____

(Use as few words as possible.)

I repeated this procedure _____ times to make certain that my results were valid.

The RESULTS were _____

_____.

The results showed that my hypothesis was _____.

                                    (supported or **not supported)**

The CONCLUSION I reached was _____

_____

_____.

*(If your hypothesis was **supported**, restate your hypothesis. If your hypothesis was **not supported**, state your revised hypothesis.)*

If I were to do this investigation again, I would _____

_____.

(Write in something you might change, or do differently.)

MAKE THEM LOOK!

The TITLE of your Science Fair project is the first thing people see when they look at your display!

You can use your QUESTION for your title. Many people do. But your project will look more interesting if you choose a "catchy" title. People will want to come to your display because they are curious!

EXAMPLE - You can use the title "FEEL THE BEAT!" for a project that has as its question: "Will listening to loud music make the heart beat faster than listening to soft music?"

Match these titles with their questions ➡️

> **PRETTY PENNY**
> **HELP! I'M FALLING!**
> **BUBBLE UP!**

1. Which dish soap makes the most bubbles?

   TITLE: _____

2. How far can a person lean without falling?

   TITLE: _____

3. What kind of juice cleans pennies best?

   TITLE: _____

Here are more questions. **You** make up a catchy title for each.

1. Does a ball roll faster on grass or dirt?

   TITLE: _____

2. Do ants like sugar or cheese better?

   TITLE: _____

3. What types of things do magnets attract?

   TITLE: _____

Your **SCIENCE PROJECT DISPLAY** should do two things:

SHOW and TELL

SHOW

Your display should catch the viewer's attention so he or she will want to look more closely at your display.

TELL

Your display should explain to the viewer what you did and what you learned in your investigation.

Here are the STEPS you should follow to make your SCIENCE PROJECT DISPLAY.

1. MAKE SURE . . .

MAKE SURE YOUR SCIENCE PROJECT REPORT HAS BEEN APPROVED by your teacher. All the information that is in your report will be on your display board. You want to be sure that everything — spelling, grammar, and content — has been checked for accuracy.

2. START THINKING . . .

START THINKING ABOUT YOUR DISPLAY. Don't wait until the last minute to begin working on it. A good display takes a good deal of time and effort.

3. PLAN OUT YOUR IDEAS . . .

PLAN OUT YOUR IDEAS on paper. Decide which things you will put on your board and *in front of* your board to make your display interesting and informative.

On your board you may want to use charts, graphs, photographs, or other illustrations, in addition to the basic information from your report. Your journal may also be placed on the board if a pocket is constructed to hold it.

In front of your board you may want to display models, or the actual materials and equipment used in your investigation. If anything is too large to put in front of your board, consider making a scaled-down model of it.

You may also want to give the viewer something to do at your display. If there is something from your investigation - a demonstration of a basic principle, a test, or an activity - that others would have fun doing, set it up in front of your board. Just make sure it is something simple, quick, and safe to do.

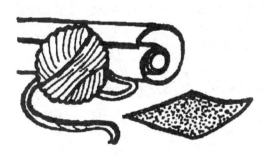

4. SELECT THE MATERIALS . . .

SELECT THE MATERIALS you will be using for the title, main sections, and backgrounds of your display. Some materials you can use are yarn, rope, string, sandpaper, construction paper, cardboard, plastic, metallic paper, burlap, carpet, wallpaper, poster board, foil, felt, flannel, cloth, cork, screen, and egg cartons.

5. DO YOUR LETTERING . . .

DO YOUR LETTERING for each main section — QUESTION, HYPOTHESIS, PROCEDURE, RESULTS, and CONCLUSION — on separate pieces of paper, tagboard, or other material.

Use a dark-colored felt-tip pen for most of your lettering — but only *after* you have printed your letters lightly with pencil. Make sure your lettering is uncrowded and easy to read. Don't use lined paper for your project. To keep your lettering straight, draw light pencil lines with a ruler. The lines can easily be erased when you are done printing with the felt-tip pen. If you draw them lightly enough, you won't even *have* to erase them.

6. ASSEMBLE YOUR DISPLAY . . .

ASSEMBLE YOUR DISPLAY by first covering your board with the background material(s) you have selected. Generally, if you have a board with hinges, don't cover the hinges. Do each panel of the board individually. Make sure all tape is secure and not showing.

Arrange everything on your board. Allow room for your title, as well as for the height and shape of anything else that will be displayed in front of your board, so nothing on the board will be blocked from view. Then, when you have all the pieces of your display board just the way you want them, you can attach them with glue.

Make your title easy to read. It should be larger than the other lettering, and should only be one to five words. You should be able to see the title of your project from quite a distance. Look at magazines, posters, and billboards to give you ideas for how you can make your title stand out.

Arrange the items that will go in front of your board, and label them with folded cards.

Be sure nothing displayed in front of your board extends over the edge of the table or the counter that is holding the board. Not only will it look bad, but someone may accidentally knock it over. You will need to have appropriate containers for liquids and other things which may leak, spill, break, or get lost. Liquids are best kept in sealable containers. Small, loose items will need to be kept in containers as well, or attached securely to a larger surface.

7. HAVE A BOX . . .

HAVE A BOX TO GO ALONG WITH YOUR DISPLAY. When your display is moved from one location to another, materials not attached directly to the board can be transported in the box. The box can then be kept hidden behind the display board, or under the table or counter the board is on.

Identify your board and your box, as well as the items that will go in the box, with the appropriate forms your teacher will give you. The identification of the board should not be visible to the viewer. Your teacher will tell you where to put it.

88

SCIENCE PROJECT

ID# _____

```
┌ ─ ─ ─ ─ ─ ─ ─ ─ ─ ─ ─ ─ ─ ─ ─ ─ ┐
│                                 │
│                                 │
│                                 │
│                                 │
│      Attach photograph here.    │
│                                 │
│                                 │
│                                 │
│                                 │
└ ─ ─ ─ ─ ─ ─ ─ ─ ─ ─ ─ ─ ─ ─ ─ ─ ┘
```

This is how my display should look.

Project Title: _____

Student: _____

Grade: _____ Room: _____

Teacher: _____

School: _____

District: _____

SCIENCE PROJECT ID TAGS

SCIENCE PROJECT ID

\# _____

Project Title: _____

_____

Student: _____

Grade: _____ Room: _____

Teacher: _____

School: _____

District: _____

SCIENCE PROJECT ID

\# _____

Project Title: _____

_____

Student: _____

Grade: _____ Room: _____

Teacher: _____

School: _____

District: _____

SCIENCE PROJECT ID

\# _____

SCIENCE PROJECT ID

\# _____

SCIENCE PROJECT ID

\# _____

SCIENCE PROJECT ID

\# _____

SCIENCE PROJECT ID

\# _____

SCIENCE PROJECT ID

\# _____

SCIENCE PROJECT ID

\# _____

SCIENCE PROJECT ID

\# _____

SCIENCE PROJECT ID

\# _____

SCIENCE PROJECT ID

\# _____

SCIENCE PROJECT ID

\# _____

SCIENCE PROJECT ID

\# _____

Science Fair Project Display
MAINTENANCE AGREEMENT

PROJECT TITLE: _____

_____

_____

☐
ID #

Student: _____

Grade: _____ Room: _____

Teacher: _____

School: _____

District: _____

The nature of my project makes it necessary for my display to be checked regularly and maintained if needed.

My project needs to be checked every _____ days for the following things:

_____

_____

_____

_____

_____

_____

It will be _____ responsibility to check my project as stated above.

_____   _____
Student's Signature   **Date**

_____   _____
Parent's Signature   **Date**

_____   _____
Teacher's Signature   **Date**

MY SCIENCE PROJECT EVALUATION

What I learned from doing my project was _____
_____
_____.

What I found hardest to do was _____
_____
_____.

What I enjoyed the most was _____
_____
_____.

I probably could have spent more time _____
_____
_____.

The people who helped me with my project were _____
_____. They helped me to _____
_____
_____.

Some comments I heard about my project were _____
_____
_____.

Some questions I have, now that I have done my project, are _____
_____
_____.

HALF INCH GRID

QUARTER INCH GRID

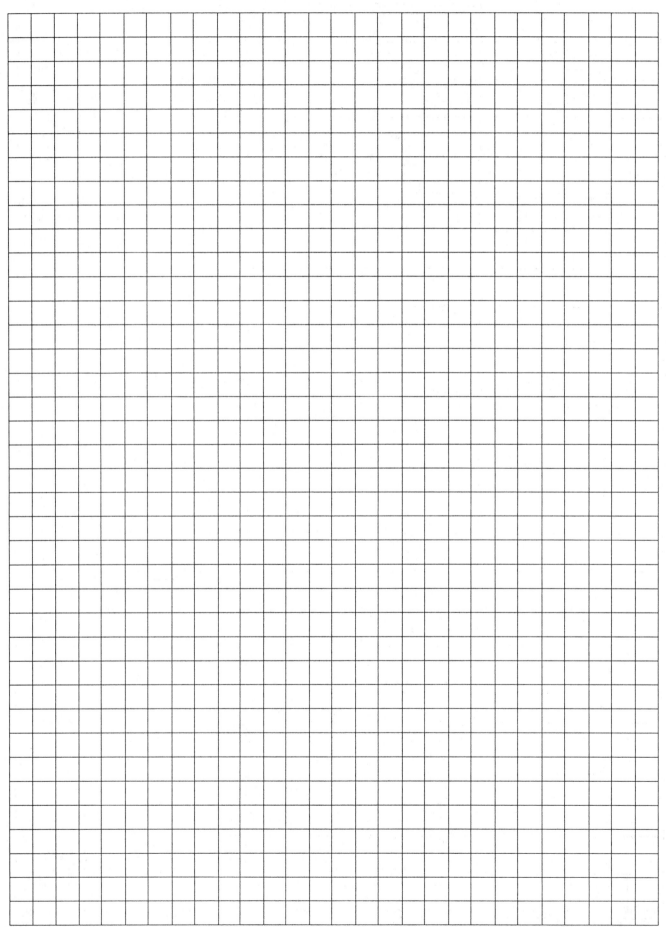

CENTIMETER GRID

HALF CENTIMETER GRID

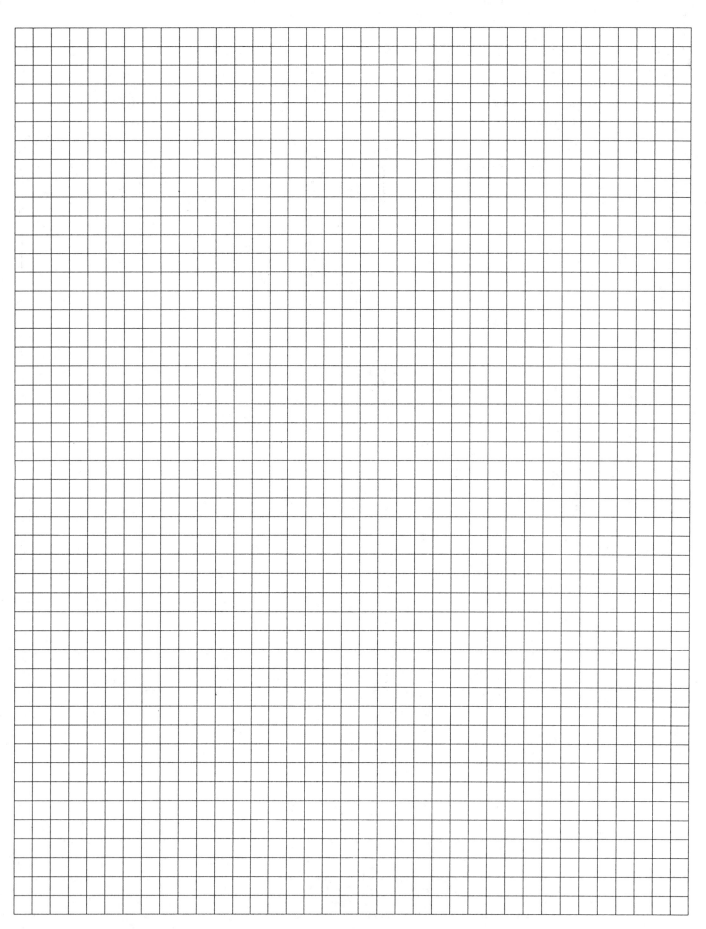